BELTON HOUSE

Lincolnshire

Adrian Tinniswood

THE NATIONAL TRUST

Chapters 1–4 and 7 have been written by Adrian
Tinniswood. For Chapter 5 Philippa Glanville, of the
Metalwork Department of the Victoria and Albert
Museum, has contributed the section on the silver,
Anthony du Boulay that on the ceramics, and Alastair
Laing that on the pictures. Chapter 6 was compiled from
invaluable work by Paul Duncan and Ros Westwood.
The picture entries were written by Alastair Laing.
Christopher Nicholson provided the section on the
carriages. To all of these the National Trust is most
grateful. For their help in various ways we would also
like to thank the following: Dr Geoffrey Beard,
Dr Christopher Brown, Mrs Judith Egerton,
Prof. Michale Jaffé, Sir Oliver Millar, Dr Tessa Murdoch,
Mrs Evelyn Newby, Dr Malcolm Rogers.

Photographs: British Architectural Library/RIBA pages 11, 27;
Conway Library, Courtauld Institute pages 7, 8, 33, 71; Fotomas
Index page 10; Howard Morgan/Foundation for Art/National
Trust Photographic Library page 78; National Trust pages 28, 32,
35, 85 (above), 87 (below); National Trust Photographic Library
front cover, pages 21, 23, 87 (above); NTPL/Graham Challifour
pages 14, 63, 68; NTPL/Mark Fiennes pages 1, 4, 6, 12, 13, 26, 46,
48, 51, 53, 54, 56, 59, 62, 65, 66, 75, 79, 83, 88, 91; NTPL/Roy Fox
pages 9, 17, 18, 22, 25, 31, 38, 39, 40, 41, 43, 64, 85 (below); NTPL/
John Hammond page 90, back cover; NTPL/Angelo Hornak
page 42; NTPL/Christopher Hurst pages 19, 29, 37, 81.

First published in Great Britain in 1992 by the National Trust
Registered charity no. 205846
© 1992 The National Trust
Reprinted with revisions 1996, 1999, 2001, 2002

ISBN 0 7078 0113 3

Designed by James Shurmer
Phototypeset in Monotype Bembo Series 270
by SPAN Graphics Ltd, Crawley, West Sussex (SG1626)
Print managed by Centurion Press Ltd (BAS)
for the National Trust (Enterprises) Ltd,
36 Queen Anne's Gate, London SW1H 9AS

CONTENTS

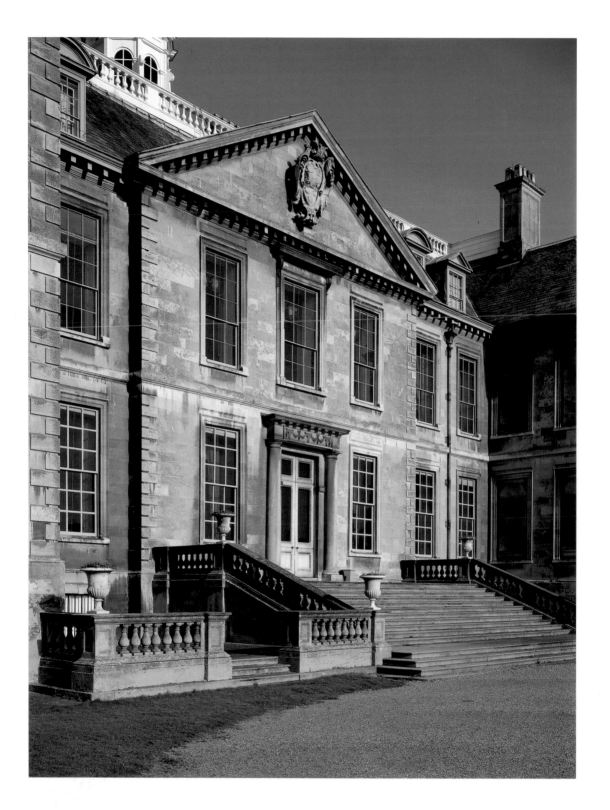

CHAPTER ONE

THE FIRST BROWNLOWS AT BELTON

Like the Hobarts of Blickling, the Harpurs of Calke and the Phelipses of Montacute, the first Brownlows of Belton owed their fortune to the rapid expansion of the legal profession during the later sixteenth century – and, like those families, they were quick to acquire a country estate with the proceeds of their law work and to establish themselves as landed gentry.

Richard Brownlow (1553–1638), who laid the foundations of the family's wealth, was the son of John, himself a successful London lawyer with a substantial house in High Holborn, near the present Brownlow Street. After entering Clement's Inn, Richard was admitted to the Inner Temple in 1583; and just eight years later he was appointed to the important and lucrative office of Chief Prothonotary of the Common Pleas, with a spectacular annual salary of £6,000. Such rapid advancement suggests important friends in high places, and his patron may well have been Sir Gilbert Gerard, the Master of the Rolls: Richard's wife, Katherine Page, had connections with Sir Gilbert's brother, William Gerard of Flambards, Harrow.

Brownlow made good use of his wealth, setting up his family at a country house in Enfield, and putting a high proportion of his income into land, much of it in Lincolnshire. Perhaps attracted by the presence of relations in the Isle of Axholme, in about 1598 he bought Ringston Hall at Rippingale and lands at Kirkby Underwood, to the south-east of Grantham, from Sir Thomas Coney. Although he and his family used Ringston for only one or two

months of each year, Richard continued to obtain land in the area, causing a good deal of resentment among the local landowners, like the irascible and impecunious Henry Clinton, 2nd Earl of Lincoln, who condemned the parvenu lawyer as a 'villayne' who 'purchased land every day from under his nose'.

Richard spent some two-thirds of his annual income, and sometimes more, in this way: in 1616–17, out of a total expenditure of £6,062, £4,706

(Opposite) The south front

(Right) Richard Brownlow (1553–1638) was a hugely successful lawyer who founded the family's fortunes and first established it in Lincolnshire; painted by an unknown English artist, 1624 (No. 55, Chapel Drawing Room)

went on land. He also borrowed or paid for his purchases by instalments, his accounts showing that he made the final payment to Coney only in November 1617. Brownlow also paid high prices for other estates in Lincolnshire: in December 1600 Henry Pakenham sold him a considerable estate at Gosberton and Surfleet, just north of Spalding, for £2,120. And in 1603 Brownlow began to negotiate the purchase of another of Pakenham's holdings – the manor of Belton, two miles to the north of Grantham.

Details of Belton's earlier history are rather sparse. It was owned in medieval times by St Mary's Abbey at York, reverting to the Crown at the Dissolution of the Monasteries in the 1530s. There may well have been a manor house there prior to the sixteenth century, although according to tradition, a subsequent owner built a new one on or near the site of the present Orangery, close by the church of SS Peter and Paul; only the gate piers in the north wall by the Orangery survive.

Whatever the nature and extent of the mansion at Belton, it probably did not figure very largely in Richard Brownlow's calculations. He was looking for income-generating land rather than another country residence. Nothing was done about the sale until 1609, when a deed shows that Pakenham sold the reversion of Belton to Richard for £4,100, after his own and his wife's death. In 1617 the Pakenhams entertained James I there during the King's progress from Burley-on-the-Hill to Lincoln. This honour so impoverished them that they resigned their life interest in Belton two years later, Richard agreeing to pay them an annuity of £560 during both their lives. Such an arrangement was inevitably something of a gamble on both sides, and Richard proved to be the loser: while Sir Henry died in 1620, Lady Pakenham lived on until 1641, still collecting the annuity.

During the 1620s and '30s Richard and Katherine Brownlow rarely visited Belton, preferring to live at Enfield. The only architectural contribution which Richard made to the property – or at least, the only contribution to survive – was the rebuilding of the church tower in 1638, the year of his death. Of the couple's six children, their eldest son, John, born in 1588, died young. Their second, born

in 1594, was christened Anthony, but renamed John after his brother's death – as a gesture of respect either to Richard's father, John Brownlow, or to Katherine's father, John Page. A third son, William, was born in 1595. There were also three daughters, Elizabeth, Mary and Audrey.

Richard Brownlow's two surviving sons were both married in 1621, John to Alice, daughter of Sir John Pulteney, and William to Elizabeth, daughter and co-heiress of William Duncombe. At the same time their father settled on his eldest son the bulk of the family estates, including Belton, Ringston, Kirkby Underwood and Rippingale, while William was given property in London and Leicestershire. Both boys followed their father into the law, via Oxford and the Inner Temple, and both were made baronets by Charles I in 1641.

Sir John (1594–1679) – always known in the family as 'Old' Sir John, to distinguish him from the builder of Belton House, 'Young' Sir John – seems

'Old' Sir John Brownlow (1594–1679) added to the Brownlow estates, most of which he handed on to his great-nephew, 'Young' Sir John; attributed to Gerard Soest (No. 7, Marble Hall)

to have led a quiet and leisurely existence, dividing his time between Belton, Lennox House in Drury Lane, and a house which he bought by the Thames at Isleworth. He carried on his father's policy of investing heavily in land, becoming a substantial sheep farmer at a time when enclosure made this a highly profitable business. Through shrewd planning and careful management he was able to more than double his inheritance, which even at the outset provided him with a healthy £4,000 a year.

But 'Old' Sir John and his wife had no children of their own, and their nephews – his brother's sons, Richard, William, John and Benjamin, and his sister Elizabeth's son, Richard Sherard – became the focus of their attention. In 1647 'Old' Sir John went to great lengths to reach a settlement dividing his property among them, and after Richard Sherard's death in 1668 the couple adopted his eldest daughter Alice, bringing her to live with them at Belton and giving her a good education. Throughout their lives Sir John's nephews and nieces and their families received presents of money from a large stock hidden away in sacks in each of his three houses. (Part of this hoard was nearly lost during the Great Fire in 1666, when Sir John ordered his servants to remove 66 sacks of coins, each containing about £100, from his London house for safe-keeping.) The eldest Brownlow nephew, Richard, was allowed the rents from Rippingale, while his brother William was given £500 a year to enable him to marry. Nor were charitable causes forgotten: in 1659 Lady Brownlow built the Bede House opposite Belton church for six poor women.

However, like his father before him, 'Old' Sir John was a long liver, and one by one his nephews, of whom he had such high hopes, died. By November 1675 he was lamenting that he had 'only two kinsmen left of my name and blood', his two great-nephews 'Young' Sir John (1659–97) and William (1665–1702), grandsons of his brother Sir William. Worried that the Brownlow family might soon die out altogether, the old man took charge of his eldest great-nephew, John, whose father had died in 1668, sending him to Westminster School and bringing him to live at Isleworth and the Drury Lane house. Both there and at Belton 'Young' Sir John must often have found himself in the company

Alice Pulteney (1604–76), who married 'Old' Sir John in 1621; attributed to Gerard Soest (No. 10, Marble Hall)

of his cousin Alice Sherard; and at the end of 1675 'Old' Sir John added a codicil to his will expressing his earnest desire that a marriage should be effected 'between my kinsman Sir John Brownlow, Bt, and my kinswoman Alice Sherard in case they shall affect one another'. The young people were evidently favourites with their great-uncle, and the idea of a marriage to unite the two branches of the family must have been conceived fairly early on. Luckily, they did 'affect one another' – Alice was certainly a very willing partner, according to a little notebook kept by her. On 27 March 1676 the couple, both scarcely sixteen years old, were married in Henry VII's Chapel at Westminster Abbey, and to mark the event 'Old' Sir John gave his great-nephew a gold watch and chain which had cost him £17, and complementary wedding rings worth £25. Lady Brownlow also spent £6 having a portrait painted of 'Young' Sir John, probably as a present to Alice, her goddaughter. Three years later 'Old' Sir John was dead, and the young couple inherited the bulk of his considerable fortune.

CHAPTER TWO

THE BUILDING OF THE HOUSE

Equipped with their great-uncle's considerable fortune – £20,000 in ready money, and an income of around £9,000 a year – 'Young' Sir John and Lady Alice Brownlow soon set aside the tradition of thrift and simple living which had underpinned and nurtured the family's rising fortunes for nearly a century. They launched into London society, spending £5,000 on a new house in Southampton (now Bloomsbury) Square, laid out in the 1660s by the 4th Earl of Southampton, and one of the most fashionable areas of the capital. And, inevitably, they turned their thoughts to the creation of a new country house which would be an appropriate setting for their rank and wealth.

A gentleman in Brownlow's position in the second half of the seventeenth century had a number of choices open to him, once the decision to build had been made. If he were not too ambitious, he could employ a local master-builder, who would draw up the plans for him and execute the work. If, on the other hand, he was of an architectural turn of mind himself, he might produce his own designs – as George Vernon had done in the 1660s at Sudbury Hall, Derbyshire – and rely on contractors to interpret and, where necessary, correct them. Or he could follow the counsel of the influential Caroline architect Roger Pratt, and 'get some ingenious gentleman who has seen much of that kind abroad and been somewhat versed in the best authors of Architecture: viz. Palladio, Scamozzi, Serlio, etc. to do it for you, and to give you a design of it in paper, though but roughly drawn.'

Sir John Brownlow took this last course, and for many years it was generally accepted that he had applied to the most famous of all these ingenious gentlemen – the Surveyor-General of the King's Works, Sir Christopher Wren. The legend that Wren designed Belton probably dates back to at least the mid-nineteenth century, when so many houses were attributed to him simply because they were of high quality and built during the later seventeenth century. However, Wren designed very few country houses, and there is certainly no evidence to support the traditional attribution of Belton, which is now thought to have been the work of his contemporary and fellow-member of the Royal Society, the soldier-architect William Winde.

Winde (d.1722) was the son of a royalist who had fled to the Low Countries after the Civil War, dying a lieutenant-colonel in the service of the States of Holland in 1658. He followed in his father's footsteps, becoming an ensign in command of English troops at Bergen-op-Zoom and, on his return to England in 1660, buying a commission in the King's Troop of the Royal Regiment of Horse. But in spite of many promises of preferment, and a successful part in combating the Monmouth Rebellion – at Sedgemoor in June 1685 he 'charged with the [King's] Troop the Green Regiment of the Rebells and totally routed them' – he never rose above the rank of captain.

Winde seems from quite early on to have taken an active interest in military engineering. When the Dutch fleet lay in the Thames in June 1667, he assisted in the fortification of Gravesend Reach, and in 1680 he was asked by Sir Bernard de Gomme, engineer-general of the King's Ordnance, to examine the defences of Portsmouth. Although nothing came of the latter project, he had for some years been pursuing a parallel career as a country house architect, largely as the result of the patronage and encouragement of his godfather, William, 1st Earl of Craven. Following the death in 1663 of Craven's original architect, Sir Balthazar Gerbier, the Earl commissioned Winde to take on the design of his house at Hampstead Marshall in Berkshire, and perhaps also that of Ashdown, a hunting lodge on the downs

'Young' Sir John Brownlow (1659–97), the builder of Belton; by Riley and Closterman (No.21, Saloon)

the windows, all indicate a common designer. There is also a letter written in February 1690, soon after Belton was completed, in which Winde recommended Edward Goudge to his patron and kinswoman Lady Bridgeman, saying that the plasterer 'is now looked on as ye beste master in Ingland in his profession, as his worke att Coombe, Hampsted, & Sr. John Brownloe's will evidence'. Goudge also worked with Winde on the alterations to Craven's Drury House, and it is tempting to speculate that the architect may have been brought to Brownlow's attention by Craven himself, since the Earl was a neighbour of 'Old' Sir John in Drury Lane. (By the 1680s Winde was himself living 'over against the Earl of Craven's house in Drury Lane'.) Nor was Goudge, 'imployed by mee this 6 or 7 years', as the architect recorded in a letter of 1688, the only craftsman at Belton with links to Winde: the carpenter Edward Willcox, who made the cupola and balustrade at Brownlow's new house, had also worked under him at Combe Abbey.

At various times in his career Winde acted as designer, supervisor of works and landscape-gardener, and was even willing to secure paintings and other art-objects for his clients. But, if he *was* the architect of Belton House, his involvement probably went no further than providing 'a design of it in paper, though but roughly drawn', in Pratt's words. Accounts and other documents in the family archives show that the execution and general supervision of the project were left to the mason-contractor William Stanton (1639–1705). A member of a family of masons and sculptors with a yard near St Andrew's church, Holborn, in London (which in 1684 he contracted to rebuild with the decorative carver Edward Pierce – another of Winde's collaborators), Stanton was primarily a monumental sculptor. He is credited with some 30 funerary monuments between 1665 and his death 40 years later, and he probably came to Brownlow's notice in 1681, when he was paid £100 to set up a monument in Belton parish church to 'Old' Sir John and his wife Alice. But in common with many seventeenth-century mason-sculptors, he not only undertook building work but was also prepared to act as clerk of works and general site supervisor when the occasion arose. Stanton is also thought to

twelve miles away and now the property of the National Trust. In 1682–5 Winde also remodelled another of Craven's country houses, Combe Abbey in Warwickshire, and there is some evidence to suggest that he did some unspecified work at his London house in Drury Lane later in the 1680s.

There are several reasons for attributing the design of 'Young' Sir John Brownlow's new house at Belton to Winde. The most telling is the stylistic parallel between Belton and the west front of Combe Abbey. The proportions of the central bays, their pediments and cartouches, and the detailing of

have designed several country houses on his own account – one of which, Denham Place in Buckinghamshire (1701), closely resembles Belton. The large sum of money which he received at Belton – some £5,000 at intervals over a three-year period between March 1685 and May 1688 – indicates that he and his assistant John Thompson (who went on in the latter year to work as contractor for Wren on St Paul's) played a central role in both the organisation of the scheme and the construction of the house.

How much Belton owes to Winde, and how much to Stanton, is impossible to say. No doubt the original drawings were revised and modified both by Stanton himself and by the various craftsmen responsible for the detailed work. But there is a third name which must stand beside those two in any consideration of the genesis of the design – that of Roger Pratt, whose advice to aspiring country house builders is quoted above. Although he had no direct involvement in Belton, the design of Brownlow's new house, like Winde's Combe Abbey, is ultimately based on the spectacular palace at the top of St James's Street, Piccadilly, which Pratt designed in 1664–7 for the Lord Chancellor, Edward Hyde,

1st Earl of Clarendon. In 1683, after Hyde's death, it was sold to 'certaine rich bankers and mechanics', who demolished it and redeveloped the site, but during its short life Clarendon House's elegant symmetry and confident and commonsensical design made it one of the most admired buildings in England. John Evelyn described it as 'without hyperbolies, the best contriv'd, the most usefull, gracefull, and magnificent house in England... Here is state and use, solidity and beauty, most symmetrically combined together.'

No plan of Clarendon survives, but a contemporary engraving of the entrance front is enough to provide us with its basic features, so many of which were reused by Winde and Stanton. Like Clarendon, Belton is a two-storeyed block with a central pediment between projecting wings, and rusticated quoins; like Clarendon, it has a hipped roof with broad eaves, dormer-windows with alternating triangular and segmental pediments; and like Clarendon, the whole is surmounted by a balustraded roof-platform and crowned with a cupola. The simplicity and elegance of Pratt's design, and the building's prominent position in the capital, ensured that other patrons besides Brown-

(Left) Clarendon House, Piccadilly, was the model for Belton. It was built between 1664 and 1667 by Sir Roger Pratt for the Lord Chancellor, Edward Hyde; engraving after J. Spilbergh

(Opposite) The south front of Belton, probably designed by William Winde, and built by William Stanton between 1684 and 1688; engraving by H. Hulsbergh from Colen Campbell's 'Vitruvius Britannicus' (1717)

low, and other architects besides Winde, sought to emulate it during the last decades of the seventeenth century. One can see echoes at Holme Lacy in Herefordshire (1674), William Smith of Warwick's Stanford Hall, Leicestershire (1697), and Hanbury Hall, Worcestershire (1701). But it is at Belton that the Clarendon type achieves its purest and arguably its greatest incarnation.

Preparations for the new house began in February 1684, when the steward's accounts show the first of many payments to local workers for gathering gorse and bracken, and binding them in sheaves as fuel to fire the brick clamps, or kilns, which were being set up on the site. Temporary buildings were put up, and – in a gesture which suggests that 'Young' Sir John had inherited at least some of the old Brownlow thrift – the old manor house was carefully taken down, and wood, stone, glass, lead and slates were stored ready to be reused in the new building. At the same time Sir John's workmen stripped and dismantled Ringston Hall, also left to him by his great-uncle, and 289 loads of stone, slate and wood were carted the twelve miles north-west to Belton at a cost of £189. Work was carried out on the grounds and outbuildings, as well: there are references in the accounts to a 'doghouse', a 'duck-house' and various ponds, and in the course of 1684 Sir John's steward paid Henry Snart '4 days sewing acrons [acorns]', and Henry Harvey '10 days setting acrons' and also a shilling for 'getting ash keys'. In the following January Thomas Everitt was paid £1 8s for 'Raleing the new plantation'.

On 13 May 1684 Brownlow's brickmaker, Samuel Truman, was given a shilling 'to drinck at the bourning the first Clamp'. However, within a few months Truman was dead, and Robert Broughton and William Plumridge had replaced him – probably, like him, itinerant brickmakers who moved on to nearby Belton Heath and set up their own clamps and diggings for the duration of the works. Broughton and Plumridge make their first appearance in the building accounts in September and December respectively, contracting to provide the site with 800,000 bricks apiece. Their rates were higher than Truman's, who had agreed to supply at 4s 6d per thousand: Broughton and Plumridge charged 6d a thousand for digging the clay, and 5s a thousand for making and firing, rising in 1686 to 5s 6d. Between April 1685 and July 1686 the two men, together with several other less

important contractors, supplied just over 1,750,000 bricks, for walling, outbuildings and the carcase of the house itself.

As that carcase took shape, the site must have been a hive of activity. Wagonload after wagonload of the golden Ancaster stone which was used to face the house was brought over from the nearby Heydour quarries of Samuel Marsh, whose son had recently been employed by the Duke of Newcastle as builder-architect at Nottingham and Bolsover castles and Welbeck Abbey in Nottinghamshire. Stone for the quoins and keystones came from Ketton, outside Stamford. Timber laths and planks, and coal to fire limekilns set up on Belton Heath, were carted 30 miles overland from the port of Boston, on the Wash, the main distribution point for such materials.

On 23 March 1685, the steward recorded that he 'Gave the mason to drinck att laying the first Ston on the new house, 5s'. Once begun, construction work progressed quite quickly, although apparently not quickly enough for Brownlow, since two months later his steward 'Gave the Rasers of Ston to drinck to make hast 1s 6d'. This seems to

have done the trick. Stanton had the shell erected and probably roofed by the autumn of 1686, when slate, wainscot and floorboards were being brought in, and decoration and finishing were well in hand by the following year. A receipt in the family archives, undated, but probably from 1687 or 1688, shows that the carpenter Edward Willcox received £90 'for making ye Lanthorne and rails and Ballisters on ye plattforme', and a further twelve guineas for 'boarding on ye platforme balustrade and cupola'. In November 1688 Sir John and Lady Brownlow moved in.

As at Clarendon House, the main storey of Belton is set above a half-basement, echoing Pratt's advice that 'an ascent is most graceful with such a basement for it looks like a thing complete in itself, and this adds to the height and majesty of a building; and a prospect is more pleasant to a house than where none, as must necessarily fall out where we cannot see over the top of our out-walls'. By siting the kitchen, buttery, larder, servants' hall and other domestic offices in this basement, Winde and Stanton left the two main floors free to be devoted to family lodgings and state apartments, with the servants' lodgings placed up in the attic storey and reached via sets of back stairs at either end of the house – a comparatively recent innovation which had been pioneered by Pratt at Coleshill in Berkshire, built for his cousin between 1650 and *c*.1662.

The visual and ceremonial focus of the house was the group of four chambers at its centre, emphasised on both of the main façades by three-bay pedimented projections. On the ground floor of the south front the Marble Hall, which takes its name from the black-and-white marble floor which Stanton laid here and in the adjoining Staircase Hall in 1687, led into a great parlour to the north (now the Saloon). Above the Marble Hall a great chamber (now the Library, but called the 'great dining room' in an inventory drawn up when the Brownlows moved in in 1688) stood back-to-back with the state bedchamber and its closet (now the Queen's Bedroom and Ante-Library). ('Let the fairest room above', wrote Pratt, 'be placed in the very midst of the house, as the bulk of a man is between his members.') The other main rooms, including the Brownlows' own lodgings on the first floor and a series of reception rooms below, were symmetrically disposed to either side of this group, the only jarring note being the placing of the main staircase to the east of the single-storey hall, rather than rising out of it as at Coleshill. But any qualms about this asymmetry are more than assuaged by Edward Goudge's masterly ceiling, incorporating the Brownlow crest of a greyhound on a cap of maintenance in the corner cartouches, bordered by scrolling sunflowers and with a garland of fruit and flowers. In 'Young' Sir John's time, the Staircase Hall had a three-fold function, as the conventional ceremonial route of ascent to the great dining-room, a recreation area and a picture gallery: the 1688 inventory shows that it held a billiard table, 'Two Sticks wth balls & Jacks' and 'Three & fortie pictures all Gold Gilt frames some being large'.

The two wings contained lodgings for Lady Alice's relations, the Sherards, and nurseries for the Brownlows' daughters, to the south; and a kitchen and chapel to the north. This chapel, again with plasterwork by Goudge, is not only one of the least altered of the seventeenth-century interiors at Belton; it is also a *tour de force* of Caroline decor-ation, a secular masterpiece in which spirituality gives way to the display of wealth, prefiguring those extravagances which Pope would castigate 50 years later in his *Moral Essays*:

And now the Chapel's silver bell you hear,
That summons you to all the Pride of Prayer.

Lush circlets and scrolls of acanthus leaves, fruit and flowers, all swirl around putti who cavort with Baroque exuberance among foliage, grapes and flowers, while four trios of chubby – and somewhat surly – cherub heads sing out from high-relief panels. The scene is presided over by two further putti who perch precariously inside a broken segmental pediment on top of a magnificent Corinthian reredos, probably the work of Stanton (who provided the marble pavement and altar steps) and the local carver Edmund Carpenter.

Carpenter, whose only documented work is at Belton, was responsible for much of the woodcarving in the house. His bill, dated 26 March 1688, specifically mentions three chimney-pieces, including one 'in the greate Parlor with fruit and

Detail of the limewood carving in the Marble Hall, by Edmund Carpenter

'Young' Sir John Brownlow commissioned this tapestry from John Vanderbank in 1691. The subjects were taken from Indian miniatures

flowers', for which he was paid £18, and another costing £26 10s, a 'very rich Chimny peece in the wth drawing roome To the greate Parlor don wth varieties of fish and sheals [shells] With birds foulige fruit & flowers'. Many of the Belton carvings have since been rearranged, and this last probably refers to the right-hand overmantel now decorating the Marble Hall. Other carvings have traditionally been assigned to Grinling Gibbons, but although Gibbons has suffered from the same indiscriminate

wave of attributions that afflicted Wren's reputation, claims concerning his putative work at Belton cannot be dismissed quite so easily. For example, Carpenter's overmantels in the great parlour (now the Saloon) and the Marble Hall both have partners that are clearly not by his hand: these are much bolder and more finely executed, and certainly show close affinities with Gibbons's authenticated work.

The 1688 inventory shows that Belton was furnished in a fairly simple but modern manner; there is no evidence to suggest that any of the oak chairs and chests from the old manor house were installed in the new building. The Marble Hall contained 'two marble cisterns with cocks', a rather daunting set of 28 paintings of kings and queens of England from William the Conqueror to William of Orange, and 'one dozen rush armchairs'. Since the Hall would have been essentially a grand introduction to the other apartments rather than a living area, these may have been for the use of servants who, in the absence of a bell-pull system, would have had to hang around there waiting for instructions, although one would have expected them to have been provided with simple benches rather than armchairs. It is perhaps more likely that they were intended for visitors waiting to see the Brownlows. The parlour was furnished with 'two very large seeing glasses', 'three crimson sarcenet curtains fringed about', eighteen more rush chairs and two japanned tables. The first-floor state bedchamber contained 'one fine bedstead with green damask curtains and valance . . . twelve green velvet armchairs . . . and three pieces of Moses tapestry hangings.'

By 1698, when a second inventory was taken, 'Young' Sir John and Lady Alice had had time to install some more opulent and fashionable decoration. In August 1691, for example, Brownlow commissioned John Vanderbank, the Chief Arras Worker of the Great Wardrobe, to make a set of hangings for the drawing-room adjoining the family gallery in the Chapel, which were 'to be of Indian figures according to ye pattern of the Queens wch are at Kensington and to be finished as well in every kind or else the said Sr John Brownlowe shall not bee obliged to have theme'. These hangings, which are still in the Chapel Drawing Room, were modelled on Mogul miniatures which had recently been brought back from India. Vanderbank's set of four 'Indian' tapestries for Queen Mary's withdrawing-room at Kensington Palace constituted his first royal commission, in 1690.

The richer decorative scheme of which Vanderbank's tapestries formed a part was carried through into the rest of the house, if the newly named rooms listed in the 1698 inventory are anything to go by. Now there was a 'green damask drawing room', a 'white varnished drawing room' and a 'white gilt closet'; a 'white and green painted chamber', a 'blue and white painted chamber' and – as at

William Blathwayt's Dyrham Park in Gloucestershire, which was being fitted out at the same time – a 'Scotch plaid room'.

But by 1698 Sir John Brownlow was dead. The serious, rather smug young man, shown complete with double chin in John Riley's portrait of about 1685 in the Saloon, had done everything expected of a wealthy country gentleman. He had built himself an appropriately grand new house; he had served as High Sheriff of Lincolnshire and MP for Grantham; he had even, on 29 October 1695, entertained his king at Belton, giving William III such a good time that he 'sent up for [Brownlow] to London to honour him the more and to require him for his kindnesses'. According to the diarist Abraham de la Pryme, 'the king was exceeding merry and drank freely which was the occasion that when he came to Lincoln he could eat nothing but a mess of milk'. Everything seemed set for the young man's further advancement, perhaps even a peerage. But in July 1697, a contemporary reported that 'Sir John Brownlow member of Parliament for Grantham . . . last week shot himself at Mr Freakes [his uncle's house] in Dorsetshire, but the reason not known'. The reason is still not known.

'Young' Sir John's widow stayed on at Belton until her death in 1721, spending her time in arranging advantageous matches for their daughters. According to her monument by Christopher Horsnaile the elder in Belton church, 'she was chiefly employed in their education: three of them she disposed in marriage to three noble peers of the realm [Jane to the future 2nd Duke of Ancaster, Elizabeth to the 6th Earl of Exeter, and Alice to the future 2nd Baron of Guilford] and the fourth [Eleanor] to the husband's nephew, out of respect to his memory'. And, the inscription might have added, out of respect for that nephew's inheritance. For on 'Young' Sir John's death Belton passed to his brother William, whose eldest son, another John, was that nephew and succeeded four years later, in 1702.

CHAPTER THREE

THE EIGHTEENTH CENTURY

Young' Sir John Brownlow's nephew, Sir John Brownlow III (1690–1754), has come down to us as rather a pathetic figure. He was possessed of a driving political ambition, but few political skills, and had an inordinately high opinion of his own importance (an opinion which was not shared by his family, his colleagues or his peers). His pretensions and his failure to achieve high office have tended to obscure a more positive side to his character – what one contemporary described as 'his nice taste and his well chosen knowledge' of the arts. It was this nice taste and well-chosen knowledge which were his greatest legacy to Belton.

In 1713, the year after Lady Brownlow had successfully engineered his marriage to her youngest daughter Eleanor, Sir John entered Parliament in the Whig interest as MP for Grantham. In the following year he was elected member for Lincolnshire, a seat which he held until 1722, when he was again returned for Grantham; and in 1718 he was created Viscount Tyrconnel and Baron Charleville, as a reward for supporting the Government, probably through the patronage of William Aislabie, Chancellor of the Exchequer, to whom he was related by marriage. As an Irish peer, he was still able to sit in the Commons, and he continued to represent Grantham until his retirement in 1741. But in spite of his lengthy political career he made little mark.

For the first few years of their married life Eleanor and John divided their time between their town house in Arlington Street, St James's, and Bruton in Somerset. Viscount Tyrconnel's own inheritance, which included the Bruton property, provided him with a reasonable income, while his wife brought with her around £1,200 a year and a fourth share in her father's unsettled estates. But Tyrconnel (or rather Sir John Brownlow, as he still was at that time) was a bad manager and proved

unable to live within his means. To be fair, this was partly because he had inherited an encumbered estate from a father who had died intestate. But the couple's difficulties were exacerbated by his love of ostentatious display, which put a great deal of pressure on the family resources. In 1715 self-imposed economies obliged the family to shut up the Arlington Street house, and Eleanor retired to Bruton with a household of six servants and a dog called Brill.

For two years, while her husband was in London pursuing his political career, she whiled away her time in socialising with the local Somerset gentry and patronising local 'sports' such as badger-hunting and bull-baiting. Her total expenses during her exile from London came to a modest £476 4s 6d (including 5s to the badger hunters and 3s to the bull baiters). The situation was relieved somewhat by 1718, when Tyrconnel sold off some of his property, including his Bruton estates. And then in 1721 Eleanor's mother, Alice, died, and under the terms of a settlement made by 'Old' Sir John on 'Young' Sir John's marriage 45 years earlier, Belton passed to them, becoming their main residence.

The Tyrconnels immediately began to consolidate their Lincolnshire estates, buying back some of the Brownlow property which had been bequeathed to Eleanor's sisters. Despite their efforts, the Belton estate remained a shadow of its former self: it gave the Tyrconnels an income of only £4,000, half of what 'Old' Sir John Brownlow had received in the seventeenth century. However, the couple were far from poor, and Viscount Tyrconnel felt free to indulge his love of the arts. Inspired perhaps by the aesthete Frederick, Prince of Wales, with whom he was on friendly terms, he patronised the poet Richard Savage, the sculptor Henry Cheere, and artists of the calibre of Thomas Smith of Derby, the court portrait-painter Charles

Sir John Brownlow, later Viscount Tyrconnel (1690–1754); by Charles Jervas (No. 51, Tyrconnel Room)

Jervas, and Philippe Mercier, whose delightful conversation piece of the Tyrconnels relaxing in the grounds of Belton – one of the first pictures of its kind to be painted in England – now hangs in the Ante-Room (No.156). Tyrconnel also began the collection of Old Masters which eventually found their way to Belton from his Arlington Street house and some of which can still be seen in the Red Drawing Room and Queen's Bedroom (see Chapter Five).

Inventories – this time from 1737 and 1754 – and bills are again our major source of information about Belton's appearance during Viscount Tyrconnel's time. In 1742 he commissioned Matthew Rennison, who also worked at Nostell Priory in Yorkshire, to replaster the ceiling of the Marble Hall, for which the stuccadore was paid £29 17s 4d, with a further £29 10s 10d the next year for unspecified stucco work on the staircase. Given pride of place in the Marble Hall was a bust of 'Butcher' Cumberland. Commissioned by Tyrconnel from Henry Cheere shortly after Culloden, this was an expression of homage and loyalty from an ardent anti-Jacobite, a celebration of 'ye News of ye Glorious & Compleat Victory obtain'd over ye Rebels in Scotland' in 1746. It now stands in the Marble Hall.

The common parlour (now the Tapestry Room) contained a number of interesting paintings, including a full-length of Charles II by Lely, now hanging in the Marble Hall (No.4); a *View of Greenwich* by Robert Griffier (No.88; Yellow Bedroom); and a portrait of 'the Grand Seignor in Ye Gardens of the Seraglio with his Ministers of State etc drawn from a copy of a Venetian painter at Constantinople'. There were also 'four plaister Figures of Boys connected to ye wainscot over ye pediments of ye doors': they no longer survive, but presumably were placed to flank pediments over the doors.

The eighteenth-century inventories show that the Saloon, then still known as the great parlour, remained one of the most important chambers in the house, and Tyrconnel lavished a good deal of money on its decoration and furnishing. In 1729 he paid 15 guineas to have the room gilded by Mark Antony Hauduroy, who had worked at Knole in

Kent for the 1st Duke of Dorset in 1723–4. In 1737 the great parlour contained the six family portraits which hang there today: Tyrconnel's father and mother, and his uncle and aunt, 'Young' Sir John and Lady Alice, all by Riley and Closterman; and two attributed to Henry Tilson of his cousins and sisters-in-law – Jane Brownlow, who married the 2nd Duke of Ancaster, and Margaret, who died tragically on the eve of her wedding. The furniture included 'two large pier glasses with three brass sconces to each' and 'two marble tables'. These pier-glasses and their matching tables are among the most important pieces in the house today. Bought by Tyrconnel, and showing the Viscount's arms set in broken pediments, they may perhaps have been designed by William Kent.

Most notable among the furnishings of what is now the Red Drawing Room, immediately west of the Saloon, were 'two pieces of fine tapestry hangings with the Late Lord's Arms and the history of Diogenes and Plato'. These were part of a set of four tapestries illustrating scenes from the life of the philosopher Diogenes and were probably woven at Mortlake. The other two may perhaps have been kept at Tyrconnel's Arlington Street house and the full set is now in the Tapestry Room at Belton.

A blue-and-white plate bearing the arms of Viscount Tyrconnel, c.1730 (Ante-Library)

The Cust Family; by Enoch Seeman, c.1741–5 (No.140, West Staircase). The widowed Anne Cust (1694–1779) sits surrounded by her children. She inherited Belton from her brother, Viscount Tyrconnel, and passed it on to her eldest son, Sir John Cust (centre, holding miniature)

As well as acquiring new hangings, paintings and furnishings, the Tyrconnels changed the functions of several of the state rooms at Belton. 'Young' Sir John Brownlow's state bedchamber over the great parlour (now the Queen's Bedroom) was turned into a picture gallery, while the room below it, the 'drawing room next to the greate Parlour' (now the Tyrconnel Room) was fitted out with a splendid bed of crimson damask, and filled with rich furniture, ornamental china figures and family portraits. In 1754 these items were valued at £250 5s, making it the most expensively furnished bedroom in the house.

In the virtuoso tradition of the seventeenth century, and against the trend of his own generation of connoisseurs to concentrate primarily on the arts, Viscount Tyrconnel did not neglect the pursuit of science and the study of 'natural curiosities'. In 1737 his 'well furnished library' (in what is now the Study) contained not only all of the usual accoutrements of a gentleman's private domain – backgammon tables, 'dice and men', a card table and a set of razors – but also a pair of globes, a microscope and a telescope, even a magic lantern 'with fourteen pieces of glass'. According to Philip Yorke, who visited in the 1740s, wooden 'books' with titles invented by Tyrconnel – *Standstill's Travels*, *Block's Thoughts* and *Dennis on the Dunciad* – stood at the ends of the library shelves.

In spite of his refined taste and his enthusiastic pursuit of learning, Viscount Tyrconnel seems to have inspired little in the way of admiration among his contemporaries. George II felt that he lacked wisdom and principle, calling him 'a puppy that never votes twice together on the same side'. The indefatigable letter-writer Mrs Delany, whom the Viscount wooed after Eleanor's death in 730, felt that even though 'he had so vast a fortune, a title and was a good natured man ... money without worth could not tempt her'. 'He had the character, very justly, of being silly', she said, 'and I would not tie myself to such a character for an empire.'

Undaunted in his search for a new wife and a son to carry on the line – he and Eleanor had had no children – Tyrconnel soon found a less discerning object for his marital ambitions, in the person of Elizabeth Cartwright of Marnham. The couple were married in January 1732, although the match was resented by other members of the family, who were no doubt as keen to see Tyrconnel die childless as he was to father an heir. The cool reception was led by his surviving sister Anne, wife of Sir Richard Cust. Her husband, perhaps sharing Anne's disappointment, wrote to her in 1732 that her brother had sold himself to a devil. He and the new Lady Tyrconnel had just spent an evening together, 'with as much ease and pleasantry as could be expected from one that detested her'.

However, Elizabeth worked hard to appease her husband's family, and eventually won them over. In the event, the couple had no children of their own – a factor which may have played a part in softening the Custs' hearts. When Sir Richard died in 1734, leaving Anne to bring up their nine children, Tyrconnel and his wife, like the childless 'Old' Sir John and Lady Alice Brownlow before them, focused their attention and ambitions on their nephews and nieces. The Cust family moved into a town house in nearby Grantham, where the Tyrconnels were constant visitors. Most of the Viscount's aspirations centred on his eldest nephew John (1718–70). In 1742 he found a bride for Sir John (as the latter became when he inherited his father's Pinchbeck baronetcy). She was a young heiress with £60,000, named Etheldred Payne, and in spite of some opposition from the Payne family, who thought that neither the Cust pedigree nor the Cust fortune was a match for theirs, the wedding took place in 1743.

Tyrconnel also used his influence to advance his nephew's political career. Having arranged his admission to the Middle Temple, where Cust took chambers in 1739, he used his interest to ensure his nephew's election in 1743 as MP for Grantham, a seat which Cust held until his death, and did everything he could to promote his political career. That career proved to be considerably more distin-guished than his uncle's: he was appointed Clerk of the Household to the Princess of Wales in 1751, and ten years later was elected Speaker of the Commons.

Tyrconnel never lived to see the full extent of his nephew's achievement, dying in 1754. To the end, his ambitions for Cust were tied up with his own desperate desire for the ultimate honour of a United Kingdom peerage, and he constantly pressed for the young man to raise the matter in the right quarters. But Cust seems to have been as shrewd and diplomatic in his private life as he was in politics, and humoured his uncle without ever doing a great deal to achieve the long-desired end. The Viscount led everyone to believe that he 'always despis'd Posthumous Pageantry', but, true to form, his funeral procession was a splendid affair, consisting of two armorial banner rolls, pairs of spurs and gauntlets, a standard and a helmet, shield and sword. Besides the family mourners, there were some 50 retainers.

Viscount Tyrconnel, like his father, died intestate. His sister Anne Cust succeeded to his estates and half of his possessions, and moved her family into Belton, making over the Grantham house to Sir John. However, he rarely used it, staying instead with his mother when he was not in London. In 1766, realising that he needed a country house appropriate to his dignity as Speaker of the House, she gave Belton to him – much to the chagrin of his brothers and sisters – and went back to Grantham.

Speaker Cust thought of retiring from his post to live the life of a country gentleman, but decided against it. He was re-elected in 1768 – the year in which the radical John Wilkes returned to England and entered Parliament for Middlesex, only to be expelled for accusing the government of instigating the massacre in St George's Fields in which the military had fired on a large crowd that had assembled to escort Wilkes to the House. Partly as a result of the controversies surrounding Wilkes, during the late 1760s Cust was called on to preside over what proved to be one of the stormiest periods in British parliamentary history. When he died in 1770, aged 51, his monument in Belton church attributed his death to the 'unusual fatigues of his office', brought about by 'the extraordinary in-crease of national business'.

Sir John Cust (1718–70) was Speaker of the House of Commons from 1761 to 1770; by Sir Joshua Reynolds, 1767–8 (No. 13, Marble Hall)

Cust had little time to have any real impact on Belton. It was left to his son, Brownlow Cust (1744–1807), to make the first major architectural changes to the house since it had been built. Raised to the peerage in 1776 as Baron Brownlow as a reward for his father's distinguished political service, he was in a good position to do so. His first wife, Jocosa Drury, who died of 'putrid fever' in 1772 after two years of marriage, was worth £103,000. His second, Frances Bankes, the daughter of a wealthy London merchant, brought with her a further £100,000 when they married in 1775.

The house which Brownlow inherited must have seemed rather old-fashioned, in spite of his great-uncle's refurnishing and rearrangement of rooms. Brownlow quickly set about a programme of alterations and repairs. In August 1770 George Sparrow was paid £38 7s 8d to repaint the house.

The next year, payments began to John Langwith, a Grantham carpenter-builder who is credited with the design of the Palladian Syston New Hall in Lincolnshire for Sir John Thorold in 1766–75. At Belton, Langwith was employed on a variety of jobs, beginning in March 1771. He took down and altered architraves and mouldings, repaired floors, replaced windows, and prepared 'Stuff for ye Seat Boards, Back & Stool for ye Necessary house in ye Gardain'. He also redecorated several rooms, although it is unlikely that he had any hand in the designs.

While all the repairs and redecoration work were being carried out, Brownlow was considering some more far-reaching changes to the structure of Belton. In March 1776, two months before his elevation to the peerage, he consulted a young man who was within a few years to become the most fashionable designer in the country, James Wyatt (1746–1813). Wyatt may well have been recommended by Philip Yorke of Erddig in Denbighshire, who was married to Brownlow's sister Elizabeth: the architect had been employed on some alterations to Erddig in 1773–4. But in any case, Wyatt had already made a name for himself with his brilliant designs for the Pantheon in Oxford Street in London, an assembly room which was completed in 1772 when he was only 26. The architect's astonishingly cavalier attitude towards his clients and his legendary lack of organisational skills had not yet tarnished his reputation, and Brownlow's choice and the timing of it suggests that he was eager to acquire the services of a distinguished architect who would transform Belton into an appropriate residence for a new peer.

As far as the exterior was concerned, that transformation involved the removal of those features which most obviously fixed the house as a creation of the late seventeenth century – the balustrade on the roof, and the cupola (which had in any case begun to leak). The roof was renewed in Westmorland slate; the alternating triangular and segmental pediments to the dormers were flattened, and the dormers themselves were reduced from eight to six on both fronts and given sash windows; and the windows on the return walls of the south front were blocked and transformed into shallow niches.

The north front, after the house was remodelled by James Wyatt in the 1770s. Wyatt removed the balustrade and cupola from the roof (although they were later restored), and simplified the dormer windows; watercolour by John Claude Nattes, 1793

Wyatt also designed a new frontispiece for the main entrance door on the south front, with a triangular pediment echoing that of the central bay above, and an entablature carved with garlands and ox-skulls supported by two slender Doric columns. In the event the pediment was omitted, leaving the entrance looking somehow rather too restrained and out of keeping with its surroundings. In fact the overall effect of Wyatt's changes to the exterior was to give Belton the appearance of a Caroline house which had been half-heartedly remodelled in a forlorn attempt to bring it into line with mid-Georgian taste – which was exactly what it was.

Internally, Wyatt's work was much less half-hearted, and as a result much more successful. The first of the four rooms which he redecorated was a first-floor bedchamber on the south front of the house (now the Boudoir). In 1776–7 this was converted into a dressing-room for Lady Brownlow. It remains one of the few feminine rooms in what is otherwise a distinctly masculine house, and it is tempting to speculate that Lord Brownlow's second wife (they had been married only for a year) may well have had a say in its redecoration. Although the room has been remodelled at least twice since Wyatt's time – once in the 1870s and again in 1963 – it retains a number of the features which he introduced, including a delicate cornice frieze and the splendid plaster ceiling. In 1777 an otherwise unknown plasterer named Utterton was paid £67 7s for his work there.

Next door to the Boudoir, Wyatt turned the old great dining chamber into an airy classical drawing-room. It was given a shallow vaulted ceiling of enlarged coffer design, with plasterwork decoration perhaps, like that of the Boudoir, by the mysterious Utterton. The process of raising the ceiling entailed cutting into two of the attic rooms, which were done away with, and diverting the old attic passage around it.

The drawing-room was converted into a library in 1876 by the 3rd Earl Brownlow, and much of its lightness and delicacy was lost. Wyatt's ceiling survives, however, as does the fine marble chimney-piece with caryatids of Ceres and Pomona and a bacchic frieze. This departs from Wyatt's original designs for the room, and may have been installed early in the nineteenth century. It has been attributed to Sir Richard Westmacott, RA.

Wyatt remodelled two other rooms at Belton: the Yellow Room, a first-floor bedchamber in the south-east wing; and the Blue Bedroom immediately below it, where today Wyatt's frieze and chimney-piece are overshadowed by the towering state bed, with its boldly architectural headboard, domed flying tester and blue damask hangings. Standing at over 16 feet high – one of the tallest in England – the bed has a complicated history, which is explained on p. 55. It is not clear whether it was installed in the Blue Bedroom as part of Wyatt's 1778 scheme, but on balance, the likelihood is that it was not: its height is such that it disrupts the delicate cornice frieze, and one would expect Wyatt to have integrated such a dominant piece of furniture into his designs in a more harmonious fashion.

Lord Brownlow's modernisation of Belton continued until the end of the century. Throughout the late 1770s and 1780s John Langwith was employed, not only in implementing some of Wyatt's alterations, but also on a host of other jobs, from hanging new sashes and putting up pictures to laying new floors and 'oltering a Bell in drawing room & Caseing ye Wier to Bells in Passage'. The painter George Sparrow also seems to have been a constant visitor to the house. A series of bills, dated between 1780 and 1798, show his men engaged in painting almost everything in the house – walls, windows and doors, '2 Large picture frame[s] ... filling up all the Worm Holes with Black puty and varnishing &c', and even 'Writing and Gilding 5 Sentences Over the Communion Table' in the church and 'Painting and Writing a Board for the Market Cart'.

At the same time, Brownlow was installing stoves and a water closet in the house, buying in new furniture and adding to the already distinguished collection of paintings. He commissioned portraits of both his wives, from Benjamin West and

One of Wyatt's 1778 designs for the ceiling of the Library (then a drawing-room)

Catherine Read, and acquired through his marriage to Frances Bankes an important group of pictures, mainly by artists of the Northern Schools (see Chapter Five). Like his relative Philip Yorke of Erddig, in the early 1770s he patronised the popular cabinetmaker Thackwaite ('Chair Work & Upholstery Work in General, at Reasonable Rates'), as well as purchasing over a thousand pounds worth of furniture from a Comte Maltzan in 1771. By the time of Brownlow's death in 1807, Belton had been well and truly dragged into the nineteenth century, its surviving Caroline decoration somewhat at odds with the elegance and convenience of its Georgian interiors. But there were more changes to come.

CHAPTER FOUR
THE NINETEENTH AND TWENTIETH CENTURIES

The new owner of Belton was the 1st Lord Brownlow's eldest son John (1779–1853), who in 1815 was created Earl Brownlow and Viscount Alford. As with so many of his class who reached manhood in the years following the French Revolution, the memory of rebellion abroad and the prospect of insurrection at home only led the 1st Earl to a more deeply entrenched belief in the existing social hierarchy, and to a determination to resist reform. After an inspection of Lincoln Castle Gaol in his role as Lord Lieutenant of Lincolnshire, he is said to have described what was one of the bleakest establishments of its time as far too much 'like a palace'. And in 1831, when the Lords threw out the Reform Bill that sought to widen the franchise, he set to to defend Belton against possible attack by rioters. A household militia was sworn in, drilled and put on watch, but the expected attack never came.

Autocratic and authoritarian, the 1st Earl was also an erudite and cultured man. He supported the excavation of Roman remains in the vicinity of Belton park – an act which caused J. P. Neale, in his *Views of Seats* (1819), to describe him as 'an accomplished and polite scholar'. His taste for the antique led him to tour Italy with the classical scholar John Chetwode Eustace in 1802, and to correspond with the antiquary Edward Dodwell, whose *Classical and Topographical Tour Through Greece* appeared in 1819. He was also a patron of contemporary artists, including Antonio Canova and Sir Richard Westmacott. Following the death in 1814 of his first wife Sophia Hume, and after advice from Westmacott, he commissioned Canova to produce the enormous statue of Religion which forms the centrepiece of her memorial in Belton church. The statue, which had been promised for 1816, had still not been delivered two years later, when Dodwell wrote from Rome that 'I am happy to inform you that it is one of his finest works, and the marble is beautiful, and is drawing towards its conclusion, and he [Canova] appeared anxious to have it as soon as possible in this country . . .' In 1826 Westmacott designed the monument to the 1st Earl's second wife, Caroline.

Like his father before him, the 1st Earl was swift to introduce new changes to Belton, and, again like his father, he chose a Wyatt as his architect. Jeffry Wyatt (1766–1840), the nephew of James, is perhaps best known today for his drastic remodelling of Windsor Castle in Berkshire (1824–40), which earned him a knighthood, the motto 'Windsor', and a change of name to Wyatville. But already in 1809, when Brownlow commissioned the first in a series of alterations to the house and grounds at Belton, Jeffry had built up a successful country house practice, providing mainly Tudor-Gothic and Elizabethan designs for an aristocratic clientele. Described by contemporaries as being 'of low stature and inelegant personal form' and 'no gentleman, vulgar minded . . . a great boaster', he possessed little of his uncle's flair for architectural drama and incident, but made up for this with diligence and dependability – qualities which were conspicuously lacking in James Wyatt's practice.

Wyatville's work at Belton, which covers the years 1809–20, included the creation of the present Orangery, designed in 1811 but not put up until c.1819, after a lull in the building works caused by the death of Sophia Brownlow in 1814, the Lion Exedra (1820), and a brewhouse on the south side of the stable courtyard. The 1st Earl also seems to have toyed with the idea of reorienting the main house – one of Jeffry's surviving drawings shows the east

(Opposite) The future 1st Earl Brownlow (1779–1853), with (on the left) his brother Henry; by John Hoppner (No. 171, Breakfast Room)

The Red Drawing Room, which still retains much of its Wyatville decoration

front with an extra storey and a balustraded roof, serving as the entrance façade, although this scheme was never carried out.

Internally, Wyatville's major work was to convert the upper part of the old kitchen in the north-west wing into a new room to house the Brownlows' growing collection of books. The kitchens were re-sited in a wing on the west side of the house, perhaps by Charles Humfrey (1772–1848), the Cambridge architect and pupil of James Wyatt who had been responsible for the initial stages of the project in 1808. Jeffry's scheme for the decoration of the new 'great library' and its adjoining ante-library was drawn up between July 1809 and 1810. His bookcases (now in the 3rd Earl's first-floor Library on the south front) may have been the work of another Wyatt – his cousin Edward (1757–1833). However, it is possible that Edward Wyatt's 1811 bill for £83 for unspecified carvings relates to rearranging and extending the existing woodcarvings. He was later employed to do something very similar to the Gibbons decor-

ations at Windsor and was known for his work in the style of Gibbons.

The new libraries were furnished in that year by Gillow & Co, who supplied chairs, window curtains, 'a handsome writing Table with leather top inlaid with metal', and '34 Green silk Curtains for the Book case Doors'. New double doors opened out of the ante-library into the Red Drawing Room, which Wyatville had heavily gilded by George Hutchinson, the painter employed for most of the work at Belton. Gillows again provided much of the furniture, as well as hanging the crimson damask which covered the walls. The doors to the Marble Hall and Saloon were re-grained; Wyatville designed a new geometrically patterned plasterwork ceiling for the Saloon – the old one was in poor condition; and he altered the main staircase, providing it with a 'Vitruvian Scroll for the String of the best Stairs', graining on the wainscot (which no longer survives) and its predominantly white and gold colour scheme, which was renewed in 1963. Other works included the redecoration of the small dining-room on the south front (now the Tapestry Room), with a cornice, a 'Rich foliage Cove Consisting of foliage Ornaments undercut' and '1 Raffled Leaf flower in Centre of Dining Room Ceiling three feet Diameter'. The plasterwork was executed *c.*1811 by the stuccadore Francis Bernasconi, who had worked at Shugborough in Staffordshire in 1803–6 for Samuel Wyatt, another of Wyatville's uncles.

Wyatville's alterations were completed by the mid-1820s, but during the decade which followed the 1st Earl contemplated further changes to Belton, consulting Sir Robert Smirke, who drew up a plan for a new office wing. In 1821 Anthony Salvin designed and built a boathouse and hermitage in the park, and a village cross, pub, blacksmith's house and cottages in Belton village, mostly in a Tudor style. By now the 1st Earl had taken a third wife – Emma Sophia, daughter of the 2nd Earl of Mount Edgcumbe (of Cotehele, in Cornwall) and Lady Sophia Hobart (of Blickling, in Norfolk – both also properties of the National Trust). Having spent her youth trailing round Europe with her uncle, Lord Castlereagh, on his official visits as Foreign Secretary, Emma Sophia was married to the 1st Earl in July 1828, and two years later was made Lady-in-Waiting to Queen Adelaide, wife of William IV. A

close relationship developed between the two, and in September 1841, when the widowed Adelaide had embarked on her wanderings following the accession of Queen Victoria in 1837, she came to stay at Belton, bringing with her the Duchess of Gloucester. 'Young' Sir John Brownlow's best bedchamber on the first floor in the centre of the north front, which had already changed its title and its function several times, was redecorated for the occasion, and – like the Caroline great chamber at Sudbury Hall, which Adelaide leased from 1840 to 1842 – was duly renamed the Queen's Bedroom.

The 1st Earl's eldest son, John, Viscount Alford (1812–51), died before his father, although, while he never inherited Belton, he was indirectly responsible for a dramatic rise in the fortunes of the Brownlow family. His mother Sophia – the wife commemorated by Canova's statue – was the only child of Lady Amelia Egerton, the sister and heiress of the unmarried 7th Earl of Bridgewater. Alford was thus Bridgewater's nearest male relative, and in 1849 he inherited the vast Egerton estates, worth some £70,000 a year. These included Ashridge Park in Hertfordshire, the creation of two architects with whom the Brownlows were already familiar; it was begun in 1808 by James Wyatt, and completed after his death in 1813 by Wyatville.

Ashridge Park, Hertfordshire, from the south-east; by John Buckler, 1822. Wyatt and Wyatville's neo-Gothic mansion came to the family in 1849 with the vast Egerton estates

The prospect of owning Ashridge – a vast and sprawling Gothic fantasy in the grand manner – must have appealed to the young Viscount, whose tastes ran to the medieval, as did those of so many Tory romantics reared on a diet of *Ivanhoe* and *Kenilworth*. Alford was one of the thirteen knights-in-armour who paid homage to the Queen of Love and Beauty before entering the lists at the famous – and rain-sodden – tournament at Eglinton Castle in Ayrshire in August 1839. He was also instrumental in providing the crowds gathered to watch the jousting with the only moment of excitement in an otherwise disastrous affair. In the final 'grand equestrian mêlée' with broadswords, the Marquess of Waterford hit him on the head, and both opponents lost their tempers and started whacking each other in earnest. The Knight Marshal had to step in and separate them. The event is recorded in John Richardson's illustrated volume, *The Eglinton Tournament* (1843), which is kept in the Library at Belton.

The Egerton legacy came with a rather curious condition: to keep his inheritance, Viscount Alford had to obtain the lapsed dukedom or marquessate of Bridgewater within five years. In the event, he had little opportunity to do so, dying in 1851 at the early age of 38. But other claimants contested the will, and at the first hearing of the case in the same year a decision was given against the Brownlow family, only to be reversed after an appeal to the House of Lords in 1853.

The 1st Earl Brownlow died in 1853, two years after his son. The family estates passed to his eleven-year-old grandson, John William Spencer Egerton Cust (1842–67), whose mother, Lady Marian, became chatelaine of both Belton and Ashridge during the boy's minority. The daughter of the 2nd Marquess of Northampton, Lady Marian was a talented artist. She pioneered the academic study of needlework, helping to found the Royal School of (Art) Needlework in 1872, and writing an influential work on *Needlework as Art* (an altar frontal by her survives in the church of Little Gaddesdon in Hertfordshire). Her London home in Kensington Gore became a centre for gatherings of artistic and literary figures.

The 2nd Earl Brownlow died unmarried in 1867 aged only 25, having had little time to make his mark on Belton. This task was left to his brother Adelbert, the charismatic 3rd and last Earl (1844–1921).

Viscount Alford and the Marquess of Waterford exchanging blows at the Eglinton tournament, 30 August 1839

*Adelaide, Countess
Brownlow (1844/5–
1917); by Frederick
Leighton, 1879 (No.77,
Staircase Hall). Mary
Gladstone was
enchanted by this dress:
'At teatime today in
white embroidered with
gold regular toga sort of
thing, and tonight with
red beads, white
handkerchief on head.
Oh lovely!'*

'Addy' was by all accounts an extremely good-looking young man, tall and handsome, with delightfully unaffected, almost boyish manners, and full of stories about the adventures which he had had while serving abroad in the army. His wife Adelaide, whom he married in 1868, was a match for him in looks. The daughter of the 18th Earl of Shrewsbury, she and her two sisters were described in 1893 as 'the salt of the earth ... they looked like the Three Fates'. In 1875 Gladstone's daughter Mary went into raptures over Adelaide, or more precisely, over the creamy-white dress which she wore when she sat for Frederick Leighton's striking full-length portrait (No. 77, now hanging on the staircase at Belton): 'At teatime today in white embroidered with gold regular toga sort of thing, and tonight with red beads, white handkerchief on head. Oh lovely!'

It was the 3rd Earl and Lady Adelaide who were responsible for what is perhaps the most remarkable of all the changes which Belton has undergone since 'Young' Sir John's time. Although they lived for much of the year either at Ashridge or at their London town house in Carlton House Terrace, during the last three decades of the nineteenth century they devoted a great deal of time and money to remodelling the Lincolnshire house. This in itself was not so surprising, but the style they chose was. They did not opt, as one might have expected, for the picturesque and lyrical Old English which Richard Norman Shaw was popularising at houses like Cragside in Northumberland (1869–84). Instead, they decided to reinstate many of Belton's late seventeenth-century features, restoring the house to something of its original Caroline splendour.

Christopher Wren, believed by the 3rd Earl to have been the designer of Belton, was, it is true, being steadily rehabilitated during the nineteenth century. However, Wren and his contemporaries were far from universally admired; and even among the younger generation of architects who rejected the constraints of Pugin's Gothic Revival dogma and looked to the seventeenth and early eighteenth centuries for inspiration – Norman Shaw, W. Eden Nesfield, Philip Webb and their circle – it was the smaller vernacular buildings of the period which

appealed, rather than the rigid symmetries and florid decoration of houses like Belton. Still a generation away was the full-blown 'Wrenaissance' of the early 1900s, epitomised by Lutyens's neo-Caroline dining-room ceiling at Castle Drogo in Devon, by E. Doran Webb's disastrous attempt to introduce Pratt-style interiors into the Palladian grandeur of Stourhead, Wiltshire (and, across the Atlantic, by The Mount, Edith Wharton's small-scale copy of Belton in Massachusetts). Unlike his forebears, the 3rd Earl made his choice of style not out of a desire to keep pace with changing architectural fashion, but out of a deep and enduring sensitivity to the spirit of the place.

The 3rd Earl's architect – whose identity remains a mystery – systematically replaced those Caroline features which had been stripped away a century before by James Wyatt. The balustrade had already been restored to the roof some years earlier, and now the cupola was reinstated and the dormers were given back their pediments. A domestic wing on the north side of the West Court was also added, linking the house with the stableyard; a modest new entrance porch was created on the west front, leading directly into the West Entrance Hall; and several of the interiors were redecorated.

The Brownlows decided on designs provided by the firm of George Jackson & Sons of Rathbone Place in London, which carried out much of the restoration work at Belton. Jacksons produced a splendid Edward Goudge pastiche with garlands of fruit and flowers, incorporating the arms of the 3rd Earl, for the Saloon ceiling; and an equally impressive piece of neo-Caroline plasterwork for Wyatville's small dining-room on the south front. This became known as the Tapestry Room, after Addy and Adelaide unearthed Viscount Tyrconnel's *Diogenes* tapestries – they were being used as carpets in the attics – and installed them there. At the same time Brownlow put up new panelling in this room, some of which came from an oak which was struck by lightning in 1875 at Brandon, a few miles north of Belton.

It was probably during the 3rd Earl's remodelling in the 1870s that the most important and enigmatic of all Belton's decorative features was installed – the rare painted floor which adorns the Tyrconnel

Room to the east of the Saloon. This floor, described as 'the finest ... to survive in Britain', has been the source of more scholarly debate than anything else in the house, and opinions are still divided as to exactly when it was executed. Several of its details, such as the anthemion motifs outside the central circle, point to the idea that it is a product of the Greek Revival, which would date it to around the time of Wyatville's remodelling. On the other hand, the fact that the Tyrconnel Room ceased to be a state bedchamber in the 1770s, with a consequent loss of status, and functioned as a billiard room from then until around the 1880s, might suggest that the floor dates from the mid-eighteenth century. A third school of thought holds that it is actually contemporary with 'Young' Sir John Brownlow's building of the house, pointing to the similarities between the Belton floor and a series of engravings for garden parterres by the architect Jean Le Blond (c.1635–1709). However, recent evidence supports the notion that it dates from the 3rd Earl Brownlow's time and that it is in fact a late Victorian neo-Caroline pastiche, like some of the existing plasterwork and woodcarving elsewhere in the house. The problem remains unsolved, although current opinion tends to favour a date some time in the nineteenth century.

Elsewhere in the house, Addy and Adelaide redecorated the Boudoir on the first floor, retaining Wyatt's cornice frieze and ceiling, and covering the walls with a green striped silk damask. They also began to transform Wyatville's library into a new 'French Dining Room' (although its 'French' character evidently did not last long, since in 1880 Morris & Co provided it with a 'new stained oak dining table'). The Hondecoeter Room, as it became known, takes its name from the huge canvases of garden scenes by the seventeenth-century Dutch artist Melchior d'Hondecoeter, which the 3rd Earl acquired in 1873.

Adelbert, 3rd Earl Brownlow (1844–1921) and his horse, 'Queen Bess'; by J. E. Boehm, 1871 (Staircase Hall)

The conversion of the library into a dining-room meant that a new place had to be found for the Brownlow books. During his brief tenure as the 2nd Earl Brownlow, Addy's brother had consulted yet another member of the Wyatt clan, Matthew Digby Wyatt, about the possibility of turning James Wyatt's great drawing-room into a library, and the 3rd Earl decided to continue with the plan, employing the local Grantham firm of John Hall to fit out the new room with the bookcases which Wyatville had designed for the old library 60 years before. Any reservations which he had about the propriety of converting the drawing-room were evidently allayed by his mother, who seems to have kept an eye on the progress of the scheme; in March 1877 he wrote from Europe to thank Lady Marian for 'your letter about Belton. I am very glad to hear that the library looks nice as I felt a little in the dark about it . . .'

Although Addy Brownlow certainly did not sweep away every change that had been imposed on Belton since the 1680s – and who, after all, would have thanked him for obliterating all traces of Wyatt and Wyatville? – he and Adelaide certainly did more than any previous generation of Brownlows to restore and maintain the original character of 'Young' Sir John's house. More than this, the neo-Caroline interiors which they commissioned have become important historical landmarks in themselves, as the forerunners of a new attitude towards the architecture of the late seventeenth century. But however important to posterity, their renovation of Belton was only a small part of the Brownlows' lives. Addy entered national politics, holding minor office in three Conservative administrations, as Parliamentary Secretary to the Local Government Board (1885–6), Paymaster General (1887–9), and Under-Secretary of State for War (1889–92). With Adelaide, he also played his part in county society to the hilt, whether it was as Lord Lieutenant of Lincolnshire, Colonel of the local militia, attending the annual Hospital Ball in Grantham, or entertaining neighbours at Belton. But there was another side to Lord and Lady Brownlow, who also moved in less earnest, less provincial circles. They were on the fringes of the Souls, that élite group of high-minded, idealistic and intellectual aristocrats, whose inner band included George Curzon, Arthur Balfour, Margot Tennant – and Lord Brownlow's cousin and heir, Harry Cust (1861–1917). The group is said to have been named at a dinner party given by the Brownlows in 1888, when Lord Charles Beresford mocked their intensity: 'You all sit and talk about each other's souls – I shall call you the Souls.'

That high-minded idealism was tempered, in Harry Cust's case at least, by a penchant for fast living. When Evan Charteris, a founder-member of the Souls, was a struggling young barrister, he once invited Harry to dinner, together with an eminent solicitor whom he was trying to impress. Cust drank rather too much, and the next day Charteris sent him a telegram saying, 'You have ruined my life but it was worth it.' Harry replied with another: 'That is a sentiment I am more used to hearing from women.'

Cust was a notorious and compulsive womaniser. Ettie Grenfell, later Lady Desborough, was one of his many admirers, much to the chagrin of her son Julian, who in spite of a grudging respect for Cust's intellectual abilities, described him as 'an old bore with vulgar hair and disgusting habits'. After a torrid affair with Violet, wife of the future 8th Duke of Rutland – an affair which the jealous Ettie turned into a short story, with Harry cast in the role of Byronic seducer – in 1893 he married Nina, the daughter of Sir William Welby-Gregory, whose Denton estate lay between Belton and the Rutlands' domain in the Vale of Belvoir. Unfortunately for Nina, marriage had little effect on his lifestyle, and Lord and Lady Brownlow took pity on her, often inviting her to stay with them at Belton.

Loose living apart, Harry Cust was extremely bright, and from an early age he was expected to do great things. A Unionist MP for Lincolnshire (1890–5) and for Bermondsey (1900–6), he was a significant figure on the London literary scene, exercising a great deal of influence as editor of the *Pall Mall Gazette* in the 1890s, and emerging as a poet of some distinction. His best-known work, 'Non Nobis' ('Not unto us the rapture of the day,

The peace of night, or love's divine surprise') appeared in the *Oxford Book of English Verse*, although it was attributed to him only in the second edition. But his political and literary pursuits were to some extent merely ways of passing the time while he waited to inherit Belton and Ashridge from his childless cousin.

That was never to be. The 3rd Earl outlived him by four years, and in January 1921 the barony and all the estates passed not to the 'old bore with ... disgusting habits' but to his younger brother, Adelbert Salusbury Cockayne Cust (1867–1927). In 1917 Harry was buried in the church at Belton, where he is commemorated by a life-sized effigy – carved by the patient and devoted Nina. In 1955, 38 years after her husband's death, she was laid to rest beside him.

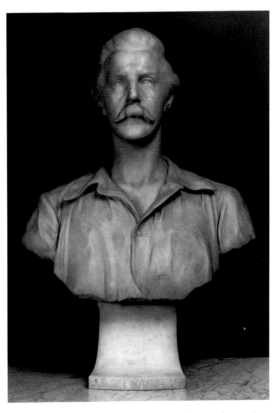

Harry Cust (1861–1917), a poet, wit – and notorious womaniser – who died before he could inherit Belton from his cousin, Lord Brownlow; by his wife Nina (West Stairs)

The heir to Belton (although not to the Earldom, which became extinct) succeeded only after some delay. He and his family were holidaying quietly in a pension in the South of France, and for some days nobody, not even the British Consul, could find them to inform them of the last Earl's death. Having lived on army pay for most of their lives, the 5th Baron Brownlow and his wife Maud were unused to the style of life which the Brownlow inheritance seemed to promise. (They did, however, splash out on a taxi to take them from Cannes to Menton when the news finally reached them.) However, that inheritance was not as lavish as it might have seemed. Land values and rentals were falling; Belton was mortgaged; and the duties that had to be paid on the death of the 3rd Earl meant that Ashridge, its collection of pictures, and some of its furnishings had to be sold off. The Hertfordshire estates were given over to trustees to deal with, and the new Lady Brownlow had the poignant task of choosing which furniture, china, glass and linen should go to Belton – and which should stay. Over the next six years, enormous cuts in staff and other savings in running costs meant that Brownlow was able to pay off the mortgage and still set aside £60,000 towards his own death duties.

His son, Peregrine Adelbert Cust (1899–1978), who inherited Belton in 1927, was destined to play a part in British history which had repercussions far beyond the walls of Belton. He is best known today, not for the country house which he so carefully preserved during his lifetime, but for his role in the Abdication Crisis of 1936.

During the early 1930s Perry Brownlow and his first wife Kitty were important members of the 'Fort Circle', often staying at Fort Belvedere, the private residence in Windsor Great Park of Edward, Prince of Wales. In his turn, the Prince occasionally came to stay at Belton, as did Wallis Simpson. When Edward succeeded to the throne in January 1936, Lord Brownlow was appointed Lord-in-Waiting to the King, and throughout that year he was his closest friend and one of his most valued advisers. It was to him that the King's supporters turned when news of Edward's intention to marry Mrs Simpson began to spread, seeking to persuade him to bring pressure on the American divorcee to

give up the King and leave the country. But Brownlow feared that if Mrs Simpson did leave England, Edward would soon follow her, precipitating the forced abdication which everybody sought to avoid. So he tried, against the King's wishes, to persuade Mrs Simpson to come to Belton instead. From there she would at least be on hand to provide Edward with advice and moral support – and she might perhaps be able to prevent him from doing anything hasty.

On 3 December 1936 the crisis was aired in the British press for the first time (although subscribers to American magazines, and readers of the communist newsletter, *The Week*, had known of it for some time). Backed into a corner, Stanley Baldwin announced the next day that the Government could not approve Edward's plan to marry Mrs Simpson without making her Queen, and to resign all claims to the throne on behalf of any children they might have. The King left London for Fort Belvedere, and Perry Brownlow and Wallis Simpson went, not to Belton, but to Cannes, where they stayed until the crisis was over. The papers began to talk openly about abdication.

It quickly became clear that Edward could not keep both his throne and the woman he loved. In Cannes Perry Brownlow pressured Mrs Simpson to renounce the King; and on 7 December it was decided that she should issue a statement saying that she was prepared to give him up: Perry advised her on its wording, and read it to waiting reporters. But the final choice lay with Edward; and at 3.35 on 10 December Baldwin entered the House of Commons and read the royal message of abdication. The King broadcast his famous farewell speech to the nation that evening, and left England the next day, while Perry Brownlow and the other members of the Fort Circle were subjected to a savage attack by Cosmo Lang, the Archbishop of Canterbury, who laid the blame for the whole affair at their doorstep and accused them of 'consuming' Edward and leading him to his downfall.

During the decades which followed, Belton remained much as the 6th Lord Brownlow had found it. However, by the 1960s it had become clear that the old house was in urgent need of repair. So, between 1961 and 1964, he commissioned the

Perry and Kitty Brownlow with their daughter Caroline under the pergola in the Italian Garden in 1936. Brownlow was a close friend of Edward VIII and played a leading role in the Abdication Crisis

architect Francis Johnson to carry out a major restoration programme, with grant-aid from the Historic Buildings Council. The roof was re-slated and the leading was replaced, and Johnson struggled to cure a serious outbreak of dry rot, which had been aggravated by a series of burst pipes during the bad winter of 1929. Panelling was taken down and repaired in many of the rooms, notably the Staircase Hall and the Chapel; cornices were cut and replaced; and a number of rooms were redecorated.

The 6th Lord Brownlow died in 1978. Six years later his son Edward gave Belton House, its garden, a quantity of garden sculpture and much of the contents to the National Trust. In addition to this,

the Trust bought the park of 1,317 acres and more of the contents of the house, and established an endowment fund to maintain the property. The total cost of £8 million was almost wholly met by the National Heritage Memorial Fund. The Belmount Tower, built for Viscount Tyrconnel in 1749–51, together with land leading up to the skyline and an important part of the village, was subsequently acquired with money bequeathed by Mr A. Oliver, with further assistance from the NHMF.

In May 1984 Lord Brownlow held a sale of those contents which would not be acquired by the Trust. Many of these furnishings and pictures had come to Belton since the last century. The principal family collections, the portraits, the porcelain, much of the silver, the complete library and the outstanding items of furniture remain at Belton, in the care of the National Trust.

CHAPTER FIVE
THE COLLECTIONS

THE PICTURES

The collection of pictures at Belton has, in some senses, come full circle. The 1688 inventory of 'Young' Sir John Brownlow's house records 175 pictures, concentrated, interestingly, on the two main staircases. Their subjects are never specified, apart from the 'Eight and Twentie pictures of Kings and Queens' in the Marble Hall (a survival of the kind of set already found in long galleries in the sixteenth century), but they seem to have been almost exclusively family portraits. Of more than 200 pictures on view today, by far the largest number are still portraits, most – and certainly the best – dating from the late seventeenth century. Lely, Wissing, Riley, Closterman, Tilson and Kneller are all represented, often by full-length portraits, showing to the full their ability to set poses and deploy drapery, to create something of aesthetic appeal beyond mere 'phiz-painting'.

Of the paintings that came to Belton in the next three centuries, one can only exclaim, as in the Book of Samuel, 'Ichabod – the glory is departed'. Viscount Tyrconnel and Sir Henry Bankes's pictures hung here, also part of Sir Abraham Hume's historic collection. Fragments remain, but most have been sold in this century. Even more tantalisingly, the outstanding collection of the 3rd Duke of Bridgewater (including masterpieces by Titian now on loan to the National Gallery of Scotland) might have come to the Brownlows with Ashridge, if the collection had been entailed. In the event the family inherited only a portion of the portraits, some of which can still be seen at Belton.

Viscount Tyrconnel followed contemporary practice in hanging the greater part of his decidedly eclectic, and erratically attributed, collection of Old Masters (152 pictures in 1738) in his London house. However, a few were at Belton, along with the family portraits (196 pictures in all in 1737). The Old Masters were probably acquired mostly from dealers. The essential passivity of Tyrconnel's mode of collecting is illustrated by a letter of thanks to his sister Lady Cust for a now untraceable portrait by Highmore of her second son, William, that she had sent to Belton in 1747:

Att my comeing home yesterday from Hanby, I was most Agreably Surpriz'd by a Box, Carryage pay'd from London, that seem'd to be a Picture, my Wife & I knowing nothing of itt, She fancy'd some of my Picture Marchants in London had sent itt unbespoke & I believe she thought itt Count Viani, but I was sure itt could not be him, when itt was Carriage payd. We were soon most Agreably undeceiv'd by finding it the Picture of my most Gallant Nephew Captain Cust. Itt now Hangs in my Wife's Dressing Room & is the most Valuable Peice of Furniture in my House & I have made our Common Ancestor the Prothonotary Give way to him . . .

Tyrconnel's greatest achievement was as a patron rather than a collector: the Mercier portrait of Tyrconnel and his kin (No. 156, Ante-room) is an important early example of the conversation piece and of the French Rococo style in England. After his death, Tyrconnel's pictures were moved to Belton, which passed to his sister, Anne, Lady Cust. A list taken by a certain Mr Patch after her death in 1779 shows them concentrated into just three rooms. Many are distinguished by fine English eighteenth-century gilded carved-wood frames.

Anne Cust's grandson and his wife, the 1st Lord and Lady Brownlow, brought the next significant increment to Belton – pictures collected by the latter's father, Sir Henry Bankes (d.1774) at his house in Wimbledon. Bankes had ranged further afield than Tyrconnel in collecting them (as far as Antwerp in 1754), and there was a corresponding enhancement of quality. The finest of his pictures to

(Opposite) View of a Terrace, with a Page; by Melchior d'Hondecoeter (No. 190, Hondecoeter Room)

Sir Abraham Hume (1749–1838); by Sir Joshua Reynolds, 1783 (No. 8, Marble Hall). Hume was an important collector of Old Masters and a pioneer art historian. His collection came into the family through his daughter, Sophia, who married the future 1st Earl Brownlow

have left Belton is Boucher's early *La vie champêtre*, which was bought in 1756. The best still here is probably the *Jan van den Wouwer* (No. 159, Ante-room), bought as a Van Dyck in 1754, and still, tentatively, attributed to him.

The final collection to come, at least in part, to Belton was the most important, that of the 1st Earl Brownlow's father-in-law, Sir Abraham Hume, 2nd Bt (1749–1838). It was also through Hume, who had married the sister of the last two Earls of Bridgewater, that the tremendous Bridgewater inheritance, including Ashridge Park, was to come to the Brownlows. Hume early gave up a political career to devote himself to the collection and study, not just of pictures, but of minerals. He was thus not only a director of the British Institution, founded in 1806 to inspire living artists by annual exhibitions of Old Masters, but also one of the founders of the Geological Society. Sir Joshua Reynolds was a friend, who painted him three times (see No. 8,

Marble Hall) and left him the pick of his Claudes. He wrote on art, publishing one of the first serious studies of Titian, in 1829, and was even an occasional artist (see No. 153, Ante-room).

Hume bought Italian pictures chiefly, at first through the dealer Robert Patoun, and subsequently directly from Italy. From Venice came Giovanni Bellini's celebrated *Portrait of a Condottiere* in 1786 (sold in 1923; now in the National Gallery of Art, Washington); from Florence in 1787 the *Madonna and Child* attributed to Fra Bartolomeo (No. 36, Ante-Room). Following the revolutionary upheavals in Europe he was able to acquire such masterpieces as Titian's *Death of Actaeon* from the Orléans collection in 1799 (sold in 1919; National Gallery, London). Hume bought fewer Northern pictures, but his purchases were distinguished; they included Rembrandt's *Aristotle Contemplating the Bust of Homer* (sold in 1893; now in the Metropolitan Museum, New York). Sadly, few of these came to Belton from Ashridge, or have remained at the house, if they did. An exception is the *Portrait of a Jew* (No. 33, Red Drawing Room), now attributed to Salomon Koninck.

While much came to Belton by inheritance, the Brownlows continued to be patrons and collectors in their own right, notably the 3rd Earl Brownlow, who was a trustee of the National Gallery from 1897. He was painted by G. F. Watts (No. 179, Breakfast Room), and commissioned the ethereal portrait of his wife by Lord Leighton (No. 77), which hangs on the stairs. He also acquired the remarkable ensemble of paintings by Hondecoeter (Nos 188–190). These have been preserved at Belton, perhaps thanks mostly to their sheer size and incorporation into the panelling of a room, but many of the finest paintings were sold, particularly after Ashridge was given up on the death of the last Earl in 1921, when the 5th and 6th Barons retrenched at Belton. More went in the sale that accompanied the transfer of the house in 1984, when the National Trust, whilst determined to retain all the portraits, could afford to buy only a token quantity of lesser Old Masters to furnish the Red Drawing Room and the Queen's Bedroom, and to indicate the various strands of collecting that had once enriched the house.

One permanent record of the collections at Belton in their heyday is the manuscript catalogue drawn up by the Hon. Elizabeth Cust, daughter of the 1st Baron Brownlow, in 1805–6. This pioneering work not only lists the pictures, but sets out their provenance and attempts to put each artist in his or her historical context. Corresponding to the catalogue, little parchment labels with the essential details were affixed to the back of each picture. With characteristic modesty she included her own works amongst the final section, by 'Artists unknown'.

THE PORCELAIN

The porcelain at Belton is of particular interest to a student of the English country house, as it is a fine cross-section of what one would hope to find in a house of its size and date. It falls into three categories – late seventeenth- and very early eighteenth-century Japanese and Chinese wares, mid-eighteenth-century English porcelain and Chinese *famille rose*, and late eighteenth-century and very early nineteenth-century Sèvres, Paris and Meissen porcelain.

Much of the early porcelain is Japanese, painted in a basic palette of red, blue and gold, and commonly known as Imari after the port in southern Japan near where it was made. The most notable example is the large bowl on the lacquer cabinet in the Ante-Library. The Imari wares mostly date from between 1690 and 1720, and are intermingled with a number of almost indistinguishable Chinese copies made between 1710 and 1730, for example the bowl in the recessed Ante-Library cabinet to the left of the door to the Library. Japanese export porcelain was popular in many European stately homes in the early eighteenth century, but we have no record of what type of porcelain was bought for Belton when it was first furnished. While some of these pieces could have been here since the beginning of the eighteenth century, many came to the house from Cockayne Hatley, the 5th Lord Brownlow's family home in Bedfordshire, when he inherited Belton in 1921.

Among the fine Japanese pieces are a number of interesting shapes, such as the barbers' bowls in the Blue Bedroom and the fan-shaped dishes in the free-standing cabinet in the Ante-Library. There are bottle-shaped vases in the Chapel Drawing Room and the Saloon, probably originally intended for

A late seventeenth-century Japanese Imari bowl (Ante-Library)

sprinkling rose-water. The Saloon also has a pair of large late seventeenth-century baluster vases and a pair of waisted beakers originally from a garniture of five pieces. In the Ante-Library there are two square vases of Kakiemon type shaped like Dutch gin bottles and painted with birds and flowering plants. The palette, which includes a brown, suggests that they were decorated at a rival kiln to the Kakiemons, *c*.1680.

Among the earliest Chinese pieces is an incense burner in the Tyrconnel Room painted in blue and white and modelled as a fabulous lion, dating from the period of the late Ming emperor Wanli (*c*.1600). In the same room is a pair of baluster vases and covers painted in the style known by the Chinese as 'Wucai' (five colours). These are precursors of the K'ang Hsi *famille verte*, and date from the Ming/Qing transition at the middle of the seventeenth century. *Famille verte* of the late K'ang Hsi period (*c*.1690–*c*.1710) is well represented in the cabinets in the Ante-Library, which hold a number of vases and dishes. It is interesting to contrast the *famille*

A late eighteenth-century Chinese cloisonné enamel quail with detachable wings (Chinese Bedroom)

verte colours with the Kakiemon enamels of the vases mentioned above and the two dishes in the same cabinets. The *famille verte* pieces match well the Chinese wallpaper in the Chinese Bedroom, which also has an amusing pair of late eighteenth-century *cloisonné* enamel quail with detachable wings forming boxes. The very tall vases on the Library chimney-piece are also *famille verte*, but with powder-blue grounds. Further large powder-blue pieces of the K'ang Hsi period are to be seen in the Queen's Bedroom and in the Red Drawing Room.

The Marble Hall has some of the finest examples of the Chinese blue-and-white porcelain in the house, including a pair of massive baluster vases and covers. On one of the chimney-pieces is a very interesting blue-and-white slender baluster vase delicately painted with birds on branches. This is of identical design to the famous pair of *famille verte* vases at Ascott in Buckinghamshire. The smaller pair of large blue-and-white baluster vases has the less usual addition of copper-red underglaze decoration. The Tapestry Room boasts a complete garniture of five K'ang Hsi blue-and-white pieces, typically used to decorate the corner fireplace. Of particular interest is a composite vase in the Ante-Library: a Chinese *café-au-lait* triple gourd bottle on a Japanese Arita jar, which itself stands on a Chinese blue-and-white ginger jar, all dating from the late seventeenth century. Assembling masses of china in this way was characteristic of the china mania brought to Britain by Queen Mary at that period. The Ante-Library also contains a small collection of Chinese porcelain, mostly of the same date, made at Dehua in the southern province of Fujian, more commonly known in Europe as *blanc-de-Chine*.

Of the two blue-and-white part armorial services in the Ante-Library, one has the arms of Sir Richard Cust and his wife Anne Brownlow in *famille rose* enamels in the centre, *c*.1730, while the other of the same date has the arms of Viscount Tyrconnel at the top. Other armorial pieces show different connections: the dish with the arms of Cookson must have come with the marriage of Henry Cust of Cockayne Hatley to Sara, daughter of Isaac Cookson, while the tea caddy with the arms of Egerton entered the house with the marriage in 1810 of

A composite vase, consisting of a Chinese café-au-lait triple gourd bottle on a Japanese Arita jar on a Chinese blue-and-white ginger jar. This was a fashionable way of displaying china in the late seventeenth century

the Dutch-German botanical artist Maria-Sybilla Merian.

Among the most important European porcelain in the house is a pair of Bow white figures in the Boudoir of Henry Woodward as 'the Fine Gentleman' and Kitty Clive as 'the Fine Lady' in Garrick's farce, *Lethe*, first performed at Drury Lane in 1740.

From the period of the 1st Baron Brownlow (1744–1807) there is a small collection of Sèvres porcelain, including seven unusual pieces with black grounds in the Yellow Bedroom. These are decorated in platinum and gold in imitation of oriental lacquer with chinoiserie figures, although the shapes are typical of the 1780 period. The Windsor Bedroom has further Sèvres and Paris cups and saucers, perhaps a harlequin coffee service, each piece decorated differently and dating from about 1800, as well as part of a Meissen (Marcolini) breakfast service of the same period, striped in pale green and gold. Finally, the late nineteenth century is well represented by a large Minton dinner service painted with the Brownlow crest, which is now in the Flower Room.

THE SILVER

The Plate Room created by the Trust is one of the unexpected pleasures of a visit to Belton. The silver embodies the personal and official high points in the history of the Brownlow and Cust families, and although reduced from its former splendour, is astonishingly rich and varied; it is strongest at three periods – the late seventeenth century, the 1760s and the Regency.

According to the 1698 inventory taken after his death, 'Young' Sir John had a handsome and valuable collection of plate. It was headed by his gold cup and personal cutlery, a luxury normally found only at royal and noble tables. His set of gilt display plate for the sideboard is now represented by the waterbottles (also known as pilgrim bottles) in the Plate Room. A generous provision of tableware demonstrates that in his dining habits, as in his surroundings generally, Sir John kept up with current fashion. Most of the elements of the late Stuart dinner service were present – knives and forks, 'boxes' for pepper, mustard and sugar, a set of

the future 1st Earl Brownlow to Sophia, granddaughter of John Egerton.

The Breakfast Room houses an interesting selection of porcelain from the Chelsea factory bearing the 'red anchor' mark of the mid-1750s, as well as a part tea service and several plates moulded and painted with flowers, and dishes in the shape of cabbage leaves and sunflowers. Of about the same date is a set of Chinese *famille rose* plates and dishes with silver pheasants within elaborate borders (Ante-Library and Red Drawing Room). In the same case in the Ante-Library as the *blanc-de-Chine* there are a very fine *famille rose écuelle* (bowl) and a pair of plates painted with irises in the style of

eight wrought salt cellars and a dozen plates. His dessert silver was gilded. To supplement the table display, a set of dish-rings of pewter was stored in the pantry. Although the chocolate pot (stored in the Still House) was of base metal, there was a silver teapot for his wife Alice's use and a pestle, mortar and skillet for cooking. For their personal comfort there was a chamber pot and bedpan, and two sets of 'Dressing plate', one presumably the 1679 toilet set now in the Virginia Museum of Fine Arts, Richmond, which bears the initials 'AB' and the Brownlow arms.

Like his contemporary at Dunham Massey in Cheshire, George Booth, Earl of Warrington, Viscount Tyrconnel spent heavily on silver following his marriage in 1712. The two-handled gilt cup, made *c.*1725 and engraved with his arms, is characteristic of his taste for the solid, massive *Régence* style of the second generation of Huguenot silversmiths such as Paul de Lamerie. As well as tureens, sauce boats, casters and condiment vases, bread baskets and dish covers, he had 'a depond for salad . . . with sconces', which was a multiple object, presumably an epergne (or table-centre) with interchangeable dishes and candlebranches. For drinking he owned six 'solatares' (or wine coasters) as well as silver labels for his wine bottles.

The silver collection at Belton was transformed when Brownlow Cust became Speaker in 1761. The traditional issue of plate to the Speaker consisted of 4,000 ounces of tableware engraved with the royal arms and intended for his official use. All the pieces are in a restrained late Rococo style, and their forms are characteristic of contemporary Parisian silver. The most spectacular item, the cistern with the royal arms and supporters, was ordered in 1769, but not delivered by Thomas Heming, the silversmith responsible for handling royal orders, until some months after the Speaker's death. The last of the traditional late Baroque cisterns to be made in England, it is unusual in not featuring the supporters of the owner, like the Manners peacocks on the late Stuart cistern at Belvoir Castle in Rutland. Despite its size, it is less than half the weight of the Philip Rollos cistern at Burghley (*c.*1710). The service also included fish trowels, bottle stands and 'Urns for Sugar, Pepper and Mustard wth Ladles',

as well as plates, dishes and covers, fish strainers and tureens.

The Speaker was supposed to return his plate to the Jewel Office on retiring, but a convention established in the late seventeenth century allowed his family to retain it. Six years after he inherited the Speaker's two services of plate, Sir Brownlow Cust formally obtained the Privy Seal granting him possession, at a cost of £138 – a bargain considering that more than 200 items in the 1772 inventory bore the royal arms.

The impact of contemporary taste on the Belton plate can be seen vividly in the first two decades of the nineteenth century. From 1802 at least, the 1st Baron Brownlow was placing large orders with several goldsmiths, particularly the two leading retailers, Robert Garrard and Rundell, Bridge & Rundell. (The pieces by Paul Storr were ordered through the latter.) More significant for Belton was the opportunity Rundells and Garrards offered their clients to buy old silver. The Regency coincided with a marked revival of interest in an eclectic range of 'Old English' styles and in all forms of elaborate ornament, in reaction against the predominant

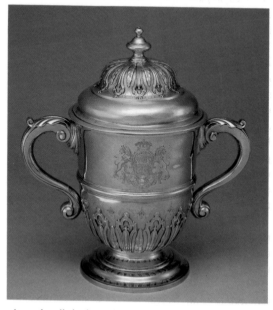

A two-handled gilt cup made c.1725 for Viscount Tyrconnel and engraved with his coat of arms

A silver cistern, or wine cooler, bearing the royal arms and lion and unicorn supporters. It was made by the royal silversmith Thomas Heming in 1770 for Speaker Cust

Neo-classicism. Several of the Prince Regent's circle employed James Wyatt and his family, as at Belton, to reinterpret these styles, and silver was essential to dress such interiors. In 1808 the royal goldsmiths Rundell, Bridge & Rundell acquired from the King at their melt or bullion value many handsome pieces of the late Stuart furnishing silver that still remained in the royal palaces, such as chandeliers, sconces and firedogs. They astutely then sold them on for their full market value to a few special clients, such as William Beckford, the Duke of Buccleuch and Lord Brownlow. These privately negotiated sales took many months and Rundells were dealing with several demanding collectors at once, so it is perhaps not surprising that some pieces should have gone astray. When Brownlow Yorke of Erddig wrote to Lord Brownlow in March 1808, thanking him for plate sent by Rundells, he added 'Messrs. R has by mistake sent in the Box a pair of sconces which from their appearance I should conceive were intended for the Chapel at Belton.'

An inventory taken two years later shows that there were by then eighteen sconces designated for the Chapel as well as seven for the Saloon, including the late Stuart ones from the royal collection. In 1819 Garrards purchased at Christie's six 'silver Girandoles' and overhauled sixteen second-hand sconces at a total cost of £111, adding 'Chas^d Coronets' to four in acknowledgement of the recent elevation of Lord Brownlow to the earldom. Sconces were, of course, no novelty at Belton; there had been some in the 1690s, but the royal ones bought in the early nineteenth century, several of which can be seen in the Plate Room, are exceptionally rich in chased and cast ornament, as were the late Stuart firedogs sold in 1963.

The heavy emphasis on ornament influenced tableware too, as can be seen in the Bridgewater dessert service, and in the borders of the dinner plates bought by Viscount Tyrconnel, which were chased around the 1820s and 1830s with Rococo flowers and scrolls and gilded for use at dessert. A newspaper account of a ball held at Belton in 1833 picked out the silver in terms that still apply today: 'The decorations of the table were exceedingly beautiful and the display of costly plate superb'.

PLANS OF THE HOUSE

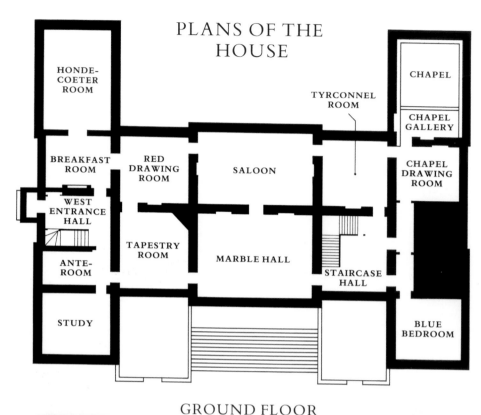

HONDE-COETER ROOM

CHAPEL

TYRCONNEL ROOM

CHAPEL GALLERY

BREAKFAST ROOM

RED DRAWING ROOM

SALOON

CHAPEL DRAWING ROOM

WEST ENTRANCE HALL

TAPESTRY ROOM

MARBLE HALL

STAIRCASE HALL

ANTE-ROOM

STUDY

BLUE BEDROOM

GROUND FLOOR

N

ANTE-LIBRARY

QUEEN'S BEDROOM

CHINESE BEDROOM

WEST LANDING

BOUDOIR

LIBRARY

WINDSOR BEDROOM

YELLOW BEDROOM

FIRST FLOOR

CHAPTER SIX
TOUR OF THE HOUSE

All the contents of the rooms are described clockwise from the entrance door under their separate headings.

THE MARBLE HALL

This is the principal room on the south side of the house. It is the grand opening to a formal procession of rooms, of which the Saloon, in the corresponding position on the north side, is the second stage. The black and white squared floor (from which it takes its name), and the arrangement of doors, windows and fireplaces, are original, while the panelling and carvings were substantially rearranged and new doors were installed by Sir Jeffry Wyatville in the early nineteenth century.

DECORATION

Wyatville grained the panelling to imitate oak. In 1856 the room was repainted and revarnished. In 1952 it was still grained, but in 1980 Shirlie, Lady Brownlow painted it magnolia and white. Oak graining has recently been reintroduced in the manner of the Wyatville scheme.

WOOD CARVINGS

The limewood carving on the left-hand side of the door to the Saloon, with its game birds, peapods and ears of corn, may be the work of Grinling Gibbons. The carving on the right-hand side is by Edmund Carpenter, who was paid £26 10s for the work in 1688. The differences in composition between these two betray the fact that they were not conceived as a pair, and it is likely that they were moved here from other parts of the house in the late nineteenth century. There are three other rectangular lime-wood panels.

PLASTERWORK

The cornice of 1811 is by Francis Bernasconi, who was often employed by Wyatville. During the 3rd Earl's refurbishing, George Jackson & Sons of Rathbone Place, London, added a new frieze and the central ceiling rose.

PICTURES

SOUTH (ENTRANCE) WALL:

1 *'Young' Sir John Brownlow, 3rd Bt (1659–97)*
ENGLISH, seventeenth-century
The builder of Belton. A much finer portrait, by Riley, is in the Saloon (No. 21).

2 *? John Cockayne (1641–1719)*
BRIAN BIRDE
Signed: *Brianus Birdeus. Pinxit Anno: 86*
Pendant to the portrait said to be of Elizabeth Cockayne (No. 64, Blue Bedroom) and therefore probably her husband, John Cockayne of Cockayne Hatley, Bedfordshire (cf. No. 145, West Staircase).

WEST WALL:

3 *? Sir Robert Long, 1st Bt (d. 1673)*
Sir PETER LELY (1618–80)
Supposedly the great-great-uncle of Dorothy Mason, Lady Brownlow (No. 25, Saloon), who was Auditor of Receipts at the Exchequer (appointed 1662) and co-Chancellor of the Queen Mother, Henrietta Maria; but possibly his nephew Sir James Long, 2nd Bt (1617–92).

4 *Charles II (1630–85)*
Sir PETER LELY (1618–80) and studio
The prime version of this picture of the King in his Garter robes is at Euston Hall in Suffolk. It is probably Lely's last official portrait of him, and was much repeated.

5 *? William Brownlow (1633–75)*
ENGLISH, seventeenth-century
This is probably William Brownlow of Snarford, the younger of the two surviving sons of Sir William Brownlow, 1st Bt of Great Humby. Possibly, however, his elder brother Sir Richard.

The Marble Hall

NORTH (FIREPLACE) WALL:

6 *Peregrine Cust, MP* (1723–85)
GEORGE ROMNEY (1734–1802)
Fourth surviving son of Sir Richard Cust and Anne
Brownlow, he died unmarried. Painted in 1779, at
the same time as the portrait of his nephew (No. 180,
Breakfast Room).

WITHIN CARVING (LEFT OF DOOR):

7 *'Old' Sir John Brownlow, 1st Bt, of Belton*
(1594–1679)
Attributed to GERARD SOEST (c.1600–81)
Dated 1644
The real founder of the Brownlow family's for-
tunes, which he left to his great-nephew and great-
niece, 'Young' Sir John Brownlow and his wife
Alice Sherard.

8 *Sir Abraham Hume, Bt, FRS* (1749–1838)
Sir JOSHUA REYNOLDS, PRA (1723–92)
Father-in-law of the 1st Earl Brownlow, and one of
three collectors of the Old Masters which once
enriched Belton (see p. 38). Painted in 1783, this is
the first of three portraits of him by Reynolds.

9 *Amelia, Lady Hume* (1751–1809)
Sir JOSHUA REYNOLDS, PRA (1723–92)
Daughter of John Egerton, Bishop of Durham, and
married to Sir Abraham Hume in 1774. It was
through the marriage in 1810 of their younger
daughter, Sophia, to the future 1st Earl Brownlow
that the Brownlows inherited the great estates of the
Earls of Bridgewater.

WITHIN CARVING (RIGHT OF DOOR):

10 *Alice Pulteney, Lady Brownlow* (1604–76)
Attributed to GERARD SOEST (c.1600–81)
Eldest daughter of Sir John Pulteney of Misterton,
married in 1621 to 'Old' Sir John Brownlow.
Charmingly commemorated holding hands with
her husband in William Stanton's monument in the
church.

11 *The Hon. and Rev. Henry Cust* (1780–1861)
JOHN HOPPNER (1758–1810)
Second son of the 1st Baron Brownlow, and later
Canon of Windsor. He took the name Cockayne
Cust when he inherited the Cockayne Hatley estate
in Bedfordshire. Ancestor of the 5th Baron Brown-
low and his descendants.

EAST WALL:

12 *Sir Richard Mason, MP (1619–85)*
Attributed to JACOB HUYSMANS (*c.*1633–96)
Clerk Comptroller of the Board of Green Cloth. Husband of Anna Margaretta Long (No. 14), and father of Dorothy, Lady Brownlow (No. 25, Saloon) and the notorious Anna, Countess of Macclesfield (No. 46, Tyrconnel Room). Cf. No. 53 (Chapel Drawing Room).

13 *Sir John Cust, 3rd Bt (1718–70)*
Sir JOSHUA REYNOLDS, PRA (1723–92)
Shown in his robes as Speaker of the House of Commons (1761–70) and painted in 1767–8 just before his re-election to this office. His wig had a sitting all of its own! Cust holds the first Bill he presented to George III for signature, to provide a settlement for Queen Charlotte in the case of the King's death. He died five days after resigning the post from exhaustion, mostly caused by the demagogue John Wilkes.

14 *? Anna Margaretta Long, Lady Mason (d.1717)*
JACOB HUYSMANS (*c.*1633–96)
Either the daughter of Sir James Long, 2nd Bt (1617–92), and Dorothy Leech (d.1710), and wife of Sir Richard Mason (No. 12), or possibly her mother, Lady Long, as recorded in the 1737 and 1754 inventories.

15 *Brownlow Cust, later 1st Baron Brownlow (1744–1807)*
Attributed to JOSEPH WRIGHT OF DERBY (1734–97)
He was raised to the peerage in 1776, in recognition of his late father's services as Speaker, taking his grandmother's family name – and his own Christian name – as his title. Painted here as a Gentleman Commoner of Cambridge University, to which he went up in 1762.

16 *Sir Pury Cust, Kt (1655–98/9)*
ENGLISH, late seventeenth-century
Father of Sir Richard Cust, 2nd Bt, of Pinchbeck, who married the future heiress, Anne Brownlow, in 1717 and so brought Belton into the Cust family.

SCULPTURE

The four Neo-classical busts were introduced by the 1st Earl Brownlow. Each stands on a scagliola pedestal.

Spencer Perceval (1762–1812), by Joseph Nollekens, RA (1737–1823), 1813. Perceval had been assassin-ated the previous year by a deranged bankrupt in the lobby of the House of Commons.

The Duke of Wellington (1769–1852), by Sir Francis Chantrey, RA (1781–1841); dated 1838 and recorded in the sculptor's ledger as costing £157.

William IV (1765–1837), by Sir Francis Chantrey, RA (1781–1841); ordered in 1838 at a cost of £210.

William Pitt the Younger (1759–1806), by Joseph Nollekens, RA (1737–1823), dated 1810.

William, Duke of Cumberland (1721–65), by Sir Henry Cheere (1703–81). The Duke's brutal suppression of the Jacobite Rebellion earned him the epithet of 'Butcher' Cumberland. Lord Tyrconnel, an ardent anti-Jacobite, purchased this rare lead bust in 1747, the year after Culloden.

On the right-hand table stands an eighteenth-century bronze group after an Antique marble of *Silenus and the infant Bacchus*; on the left-hand table are a bronze group of *Latona and her children* after Gaspard Marsy, and an eighteenth-century bronze after an Antique marble of the *Borghese Gladiator*.

FURNITURE

A pair of Regency 'Kent Revival' side tables are supported by gilt crouching greyhounds, the first of many manifestations of the Brownlow crest at Belton, ranging from the engraved fretwork lockplates of the doors to the weathercock on the cupola.

The mahogany wheelback chairs are dated by the arms on the backs to between 1770 and 1772, the period of the 1st Baron Brownlow's brief marriage to Jocosa Drury.

CERAMICS

Five K'ang Hsi blue-and-white porcelain baluster vases. The smaller pair has unusual copper-red underglaze decoration.

ABOVE LEFT-HAND FIREPLACE:

Two beaker vases, two quatrefoil baluster vases, two Japanese saucers and a double gourd vase.

ABOVE RIGHT-HAND FIREPLACE:

Two beaker vases, two Japanese vases, two foliate bowls and an egg-shaped vase.

THE SALOON

This magnificent state reception room is placed on
the main axis of the formal garden to the north.
Until the 1770s it was known as the Great Parlour,
the second in the procession of rooms from the
Marble Hall. Although it became known as the
Saloon early in the nineteenth century, when it
underwent a number of changes, it retains much of
its seventeenth-century atmosphere: the coloured
marble fireplaces are original and the ceiling is a
successful Victorian pastiche in the style of the
Caroline decorative plasterer Edward Goudge.

DECORATION

It seems that the panelling was always varnished.
During the Wyatville period it may have been
partly gilded. It was altered in 1869.

WOOD CARVINGS

Edmund Carpenter's bill of March 1688, for £18,
mentions work on an overmantel which corres-
ponds in its bare essentials to the one at the east
(right-hand) end of the Saloon. There is no mention
of the bolder and richer composition in the overmantel at the west (left-hand) end. This may be the
work of Grinling Gibbons.

The appliqué drops of tumbling putti between
the full-length pictures may be nineteenth-century
work by W. G. Rogers, the authority on Gibbons,
who worked on carvings at Burghley in North-
amptonshire and Chatsworth in Derbyshire. The
garlands over the doors could also date from this
time.

PLASTERWORK

The original plaster ceiling was replaced by Wyatville's plasterer Francis Bernasconi in 1811–12.
Bernasconi's geometrically patterned ceiling fell

down in 1877, and was itself replaced by George Jackson & Sons, who had worked for the 3rd Earl Brownlow in 1873. They charged £258 7s for work in the Saloon in 1892. The design of garlands of fruit and flowers includes the arms of the 3rd Earl.

PICTURES

SOUTH WALL:

20 *Alice Sherard, Lady Brownlow* (1659–1721)
Daughter of Richard Sherard of Lobthorpe and Margaret Dewe, married in 1676 to her second cousin, 'Young' Sir John Brownlow, in conformity with the 'earnest desire' of their childless great-uncle, 'Old' Sir John Brownlow, who settled his estates on them and their male heirs (only). She continued to live at Belton after the death of her husband, concerning herself chiefly with arranging splendid matches for their daughters.

21 *'Young' Sir John Brownlow, 3rd Bt* (1659–97)
The builder of Belton. Elder son of Sir Richard Brownlow, 2nd Bt, of Great Humby, and Elizabeth Freke. In 1676 he married his cousin, Alice Sherard, who bore him five daughters who reached adulthood. The rumours of his suicide in the midst of apparent good fortune are hard to explain. Pendant to No. 20.

OVER LEFT-HAND MANTELPIECE:

22 *Jane Brownlow, Duchess of Ancaster* (1689–1736)
Attributed to HENRY TILSON (1659–95)
Fourth surviving daughter of 'Young' Sir John Brownlow; married to Peregrine, Lord Willoughby (later 2nd Duke of Ancaster) in 1711, who had earlier courted her elder sister, Margaret (see No. 19, Tapestry Room).

OVER RIGHT-HAND MANTELPIECE:

23 *Margaret Brownlow* (1687–1710)
HENRY TILSON (1659–95)
For biography, see No. 19, Tapestry Room. Full-length single portraits of young girls are very unusual in the seventeenth century. Did 'Young' Sir John and Lady Brownlow early realise that they were not going to have a son?

SOUTH WALL:

JOHN RILEY (1646–91) and JOHN CLOSTERMAN (1660–1711)
Nos 20, 21, 24 and 25 are the four 'verie large Pictures' that seem to have been in this room since 1688. Riley probably painted only the heads; his partner, Closterman, the rest.

24 *Sir William Brownlow, 4th Bt* (1665–1702)
He inherited Belton after the death of his elder brother, 'Young' Sir John, in 1697, but never lived there himself. He was the father of Viscount Tyrconnel and of Anne Brownlow, who brought Belton into the Cust family.

25 *Dorothy Mason, Lady Brownlow* (1665?–99/1700)
Daughter of Sir Richard Mason (No. 12, Marble Hall) and Anna Margaretta Long (No. 14, Marble Hall), and first wife of Sir William Brownlow, Bt. Described as 'really deserving everybody's love'. Pendant to No. 24.

FURNITURE

Pair of giltwood pier-glasses and matching tables decorated with Tyrconnel arms, c.1740. Of bold Kentian design, they support alabaster and Sicilian jasper slabs.

Two Regency marble-topped console tables supported by carved and gilt eagles.

Two sets of carved walnut armchairs, c.1680, with cherubs on the legs and uprights as well as on the back rails and front stretchers. The panels of crimson silk velvet in the backs were probably fitted in the nineteenth century, replacing the original carved wooden slats.

Two Regency rosewood footstools.

Carrara marble bust of Augustus Caesar.

Two breccia marble urns on matching pedestals.

CERAMICS

Two ormolu-mounted *gros bleu* Sèvres vases mounted as lamps.

The other vases and the chimney-piece garniture are all Japanese Imari. The bottle-shaped vases were probably intended for sprinkling rose-water.

CARPET

The Aubusson carpet, measuring 37 ft 6 in × 24 ft 4 in, was commissioned by the 1st Earl, who visited the Aubusson factory on a trip to Paris in 1839. The Earl also ordered three pieces of carpet to fill the window embrasures.

THE TYRCONNEL ROOM

This room has undergone a number of changes since the late seventeenth century, when it was known first as the 'Drawing Room next to the greate Parlour', and then as the 'Green Damask Drawing Room'. By 1737 Viscount Tyrconnel had furnished it as a bedroom, the Crimson Room. After his death in 1754, Anne, Lady Cust made it the Billiard Room, and this it remained until the 3rd Earl's late nineteenth-century remodelling.

DECORATION

The room apparently retained its eighteenth-century decoration until the late nineteenth century, when it was panelled in oak with insets of crimson and white damask. The scrolled and gilded pelmets are of the same date. The panelling seems to have been reused and has a similar look to that in the Saloon, which was altered in 1869. The damask in the panels is machine-made and so must date from the same period.

FLOOR

The unusual painted floor incorporates the Belton greyhounds and the Brownlow arms. Its date is uncertain (see p. 31); the form of the floorboards suggests a date in the nineteenth century.

CARVINGS

The appliqué carving around the overmantel is probably a nineteenth-century pastiche by either George Jackson & Sons or W. G. Rogers, and was probably gilded when first put up. The carved frieze panel with Sir John Brownlow's monogram may be that referred to in Edmund Carpenter's bill of March 1688 as 'on frees for the same chimny with yr cipher'.

PICTURES

EAST WALL:

44 *? Elizabeth Freke, Lady Brownlow* (1634–84)
Attributed to HENRY ANDERTON (c.1630–70)
Probably the pendant to No.134 (West Staircase), and therefore the wife of Sir Richard Brownlow, 2nd Bt, of Great Humby. Left in debt by her husband, she had to contest an attempt by 'Old' Sir John Brownlow to remove her son and his heir, 'Young' Sir John, from her care.

45 *Elizabeth Cartwright, Viscountess Tyrconnel* (d.1780)
ENOCH SEEMAN (c.1694–1744)
Signed and dated 1735
Lord Tyrconnel's second wife in her robes as a peeress. Daughter of William Cartwright of Marnham, and at first much disliked by her husband's family, but later a cherished aunt of his Cust nephews and nieces.

46 *Anne Mason, Countess of Macclesfield* (1666?-1753)
WILLIAM WISSING (1653–87)
Inscribed with identity, artist and date, 1687
Sister of Dorothy Mason, Lady Brownlow (No. 25, Saloon), and the subject of a bizarre scandal. Deserted by her first husband, Charles Gerard, Lord Brandon (later 2nd Earl of Macclesfield) after only two years of teenage marriage, she began a liaison ten years later with Richard Savage, 4th Earl Rivers, from which two children were born, who were put out to nurse in great secrecy, and died. Years later the fostered poet Richard Savage (a friend of Viscount Tyrconnel) heard the story, and made a career from pretending he was the abandoned bastard of the Countess – a tale related by Samuel Johnson in his *Lives of the English Poets*.

SOUTH WALL:

47 *? Alice Brownlow, Lady Guilford* (1684–1727)
CHARLES D'AGAR (1669–1723)
Third daughter of 'Young' Sir John and Alice, Lady Brownlow; married in 1703 to Francis, 2nd Baron Guilford (1672–1729), as his second wife. Painted around 1710, too late to have been the widowed Alice, Lady Brownlow as inscribed, so possibly the daughter with her Christian name.

OVER MANTELPIECE:

48 *Alice Sherard, Lady Brownlow* (1659–1721)
Sir GODFREY KNELLER (1646/9–1723)
Painted in the later 1680s. For biography, see No. 20, Saloon.

49 *? Elizabeth Sherard*
Attributed to JOHN RILEY (1646–91)
This cannot, as inscribed, be Lady Elizabeth Cecil, granddaughter of Alice, Lady Brownlow, who married William Aislabie of Studley Royal, Yorkshire. If really an Elizabeth, she is most probably Alice's unmarried sister, Elizabeth Sherard, who lived with the family and had a room named after her at Belton (now the Bamboo Room).

The unusual painted floor in the Tyrconnel Room incorporates the Belton greyhound

WEST WALL:

50 *Mary Sherard, Mrs Whitcombe* (b.1663)
WILLIAM WISSING (1653–87)
Another sister of Alice, Lady Brownlow, she married Peter Whitcombe of Braxted, Essex. One of their daughters and her husband, Francis Dayrell, appear in Mercier's conversation piece (No.156, Ante-room).

51 *Sir John Brownlow, Viscount Tyrconnel* (1690–1754)
CHARLES JERVAS (c.1675–1739)
The last of the Brownlows – save for his sister Anne, who married Sir Richard Cust, and brought Belton to the Custs. Seen here in his robes as a Knight of the Order of the Bath, which he became when George I revived the Order in 1725, with the Chapel of Henry VII at Westminster Abbey, which was fitted up for the Order, in the background.

52 ? *Ursula Cust, Mrs Newton* (1683/4–1757)
Attributed to MICHAEL DAHL (1656?–1743)
Possibly the second daughter of Sir Pury Cust and Ursula Woodcock, 'Nutty', who married Richard Newton, Treasurer of the Middle Temple, around 1722.

FURNITURE

Queen Anne pier-glass – the pair to that in the Chapel Drawing Room. The arms of 'Young' Sir John Brownlow and his wife appear in cut glass just below the cresting.
Pair of side tables, George II in style, with satyrs and paw feet, early eighteenth-century.
The walnut side chairs are a mixed early eighteenth-century set.
On the floor under the table is a rare Charles II burr-walnut domed coffer with repoussé gilt-metal mounts and handles.
Pair of Regency giltwood pelmet boards.
Pair of Regency ormolu wall lights.
Regency D-fender.

CLOCKS

Early eighteenth-century ebonised longcase clock by the London clockmaker Daniel Delander (fl.1699–1733).
Overmantel clock in scarlet tortoiseshell case, c.1710, by Thomas Vernon of London.

CERAMICS

A pair of Chinese Wucai ('five colours') baluster vases, mid-seventeenth-century.

The blue-and-white china on the mantel includes a rare late Ming incense burner in the form of a fabulous lion, c.1680.

THE CHAPEL DRAWING ROOM

In the early eighteenth century this was known as the Blue Drawing Room, and before that as the Ante-Room. It was decorated as it appears now in 1772, when the 1st Lord Brownlow employed the house painter George Sparrow to marble the panelling. However, when the tapestries were rehung recently, evidence was revealed which suggests that Sparrow may only have touched up an earlier decorative scheme – in which case the Chapel Drawing Room presents one of the few surviving seventeenth-century interiors at Belton.

PICTURES

NORTH WALL:

53 *Sir Richard Mason, MP* (1619–85)
JACOB HUYSMANS (c.1633–96)
For biography, see No. 12, Marble Hall.

54 *Sir Thomas Egerton, Baron Ellesmere, Viscount Brackley* (1540?–1617)
ENGLISH, 1613
Lord Keeper to Queen Elizabeth, Lord Chancellor to James I, and chief legal defender of the royal prerogative. Founder of the fortunes of the Egerton family, which passed to the Brownlows via Lady Hume (No. 9, Marble Hall).

55 *Richard Brownlow* (1553–1638)
ENGLISH, 1624
The founder of the family's fortunes, in his robes as Chief Prothonotary of the Common Pleas (1591–1638). He used the extraordinary revenues of this office to buy the Belton estate and almost all the land that came on to the market in this area of Lincolnshire. Joshua Marshall used this portrait for the effigy on his tomb in Belton church.

56 *Portrait of a Gentleman*
ENGLISH, c.1670–80

57 *Grand Duke Ferdinand II of Tuscany* (1610–70)
Studio of JUSTUS SUSTERMANS (1597–1681)
Variant of a portrait of the 1650s in the Uffizi. The sitter's son, the future Cosimo III, visited England in 1669. In the original, the artist was subsequently forced to remove the ostentatiously plumed hat, because of the criticisms of a courtier.

OVER DOOR TO CHAPEL CORRIDOR:

58 *Eleanor Brownlow, Viscountess Tyrconnel* (1691–1730)
MICHAEL DAHL (1656?–1743)
For biography, see No. 18, Tapestry Room.

OVER DOOR TO TYRCONNEL ROOM:

59 *Ursula Woodcock, Lady Cust* (1659–83/4)
Attributed to GERARD SOEST (c.1600–81)
Only surviving child of Edward Woodcock of Newtimber, Sussex (1617–60), married to Sir Pury Cust (No. 16, Marble Hall) in 1678, and mother of Sir Richard Cust, 2nd Bt.

TEXTILES

The two tapestries set into the panelling are by John Vanderbank (d.1727), Chief Arras Worker of the Great Wardrobe. They were supplied to 'Young' Sir John Brownlow under the terms of an agreement dated August 1691, which stipulated that they should be of the same pattern as those which Vanderbank had created for Queen Mary's withdrawing-room at Kensington Palace in the previous year. With their combination of hunting scenes, fantastic amphibians, deities and noblemen and ladies with their entourages, all inhabiting a series of little islands in a snuff-coloured ocean, they are among the finest surviving examples of their kind.

Regency crimson wool curtains with giltwood pelmets.

Feraghan carpet.

FURNITURE

Cabinet on stand from Antwerp, late seventeenth-century.

Queen Anne pier-glass, pair to the one in the Tyrconnel Room.

English black japanned table, early eighteenth-century.

Three late seventeenth-century beechwood and walnut armchairs, two of which retain their original crimson silk velvet upholstery.

Louis XIV Boulle writing table, of the type known as a *bureau Mazarin*.
Regency giltwood pelmet boards.
Regency giltwood ceiling light.

CERAMICS

The porcelain is Japanese Imari.

THE CHAPEL GALLERY

The Chapel and its Gallery are among the interiors most representative of the seventeenth-century character of Belton. The Gallery follows an arrangement common from the end of the Middle Ages, whereby the family 'closet', perhaps the most private of all the rooms in the house, opened on to the chapel at first-floor level.

The tablet in the doorway commemorates the restoration of Belton carried out in the 1960s by the 6th Lord Brownlow and his second wife Dorothy.

WOOD CARVINGS

The panelling sets off what is possibly the finest of all the decorative carvings at Belton, with some of the peapods, wheat ears, fruit and flowers worthy of Grinling Gibbons himself.

CEILING

The Chapel and Gallery ceilings are both the work of Edward Goudge, who was paid in part for the work in 1687. The Gallery ceiling incorporates within grotesque cartouches the arms of Brownlow at the east end and Sherard ('Young' Sir John's wife's family) at the west.

PICTURE

60 *Madonna and Child with grapes*
Manner of JOOS VAN CLEEVE (fl.1511–40)
The sleep of the Christ Child is a prefiguration of his death, and the grapes of his institution of the Eucharist.

ORGAN

An important early work by the celebrated organ builder William Hill, inserted in 1826 perhaps under the direction of Wyatville. The profile medallion is of G. F. Handel. Hydraulic bellows, added in 1896, were driven by water power from the ram in the Wilderness next to the entrance drive.

An early sixteenth-century Flemish painting of the Madonna and Child is surrounded by some of the finest woodcarving in the house (Chapel Gallery)

The instrument has recently been restored to performing condition, and is occasionally played when the house is open to the public.

FURNITURE

Two of the set of beechwood and walnut chairs from the Chapel Drawing Room, late seventeenth-century.
Regency footstool.
Crimson velvet footstool.
Gilt metal lantern.
Regency D-fender.

THE CHAPEL

By the later seventeenth century the country house chapel had become, in effect, a quasi-public room of state, like the great chamber and the best bed-chamber. 'Young' Sir John Brownlow's Chapel reflects this trend: its opulence and splendour arise as much from the desire to express status as from more spiritual motives.

DECORATION

The wooden reredos was painted to simulate marble in 1892, but it is not clear whether this was an entirely new scheme or the reinstatement of an earlier one. Prior to 1892 the reredos was grained to simulate cedar, as is the panelling today.

REREDOS

The reredos screen, with its pairs of Corinthian capitals, broken segmental pediment and putti, is perhaps the result of a collaboration between William Stanton, the mason-contractor in charge of the building of Belton, and a local carver such as Edmund Carpenter. The strong design anticipates the reredos of c.1693 in the chapel of Trinity College, Oxford, attributed to Grinling Gibbons. Carpenter may also have been responsible for the appliqué carvings surrounding the crimson silk velvet panel behind the altar; they are not of the same standard as those in the Gallery. The panel is signed 'Anne Cust *fecert*, 1769', and was put up to replace an earlier panel in 1771. The characteristic IHS monogram is embroidered in a sunburst, answering the quadrant rays at the corners.

CARPET

The altar carpet, c.1830, is of an interesting heraldic design featuring the Garter star. It has been cut to fit the space.

FURNITURE

Three late seventeenth-century stools.
Six mid-seventeenth-century oak footstools.
Six crimson velvet cushions.
Bronze altar candlesticks.
Victorian mahogany card-table.
Altar table of seventeenth-century design.
Nineteenth-century alabaster bust of Christ.

(Opposite) The Chapel before restoration

SILVER

Two pairs of silver sconces. Originally made for the Crown, these came to Belton around 1808 as the result of some sharp practice by the royal gold-smiths, Rundell, Bridge & Rundell. The King gave them to Rundells as bullion for a new commission, but this was made from other stock and the sconces were then sold intact (see Chapter Five). They are shaped as scrolled cartouches, with grotesque masks with earl's coronets for the finials.

THE BLUE BEDROOM

In the late seventeenth century this room was occupied by 'Young' Sir John Brownlow's brother-in-law, Sir John Sherard, whose portrait hangs here (No. 66). It was subsequently known as 'the Room over the Still House', and it now takes its name from the magnificent bed which dominates the room.

DECORATION

In 1778 James Wyatt submitted designs for the chimney-piece, and for the cornice and frieze, which are still in place. The present decoration dates from the 1960s, when the silk wall hangings designed by Franco Scalamandra were put up. Franco Scalamandra's initials are incorporated in the design.

CHIMNEY-PIECE

Wyatt's drawing for the chimney-piece survives, although it does not show the frieze or the Ionic columns on either side.
Regency D-fender.

BED

The bed is in the style of Francis Lapiere, a Huguenot craftsman working in England in the early eighteenth century. It closely resembles a bed made around 1704–10 for Dyrham Park, near Bath, and may have been acquired by Dame Alice, widow of 'Young' Sir John Brownlow. First reupholstered in 1813 by the 2nd Baron (later 1st Earl) Brownlow, it was hung with blue silk damask, and at the same time the curtain pelmets, the curtains and some of the furniture were covered to match. If, as is thought, the bed originally stood in what is now the Tyrconnel Room, eighteenth-century inventories suggest that the present uphol-

The Blue Bedroom

stery replaced crimson or embroidered hangings. Traces of crimson silk were found on the bed-frame during the course of recent conservation work. At over 16 feet high the bed is unusually tall for the period. As originally configured, it was a conventional four-poster. The conversion to the present 'angel tester' form may have coincided with the re-upholstery of 1813.

PICTURES

OVER CHIMNEY-PIECE:

61 *Sir Thomas Drury, Bt, of Overstone* (1712–59)
THOMAS HUDSON (1701–79)
Dated 1754
Father of Jocosa, first wife of 1st Baron Brownlow, and of Mary Anne, wife of 2nd Earl of Buckinghamshire (of Blickling, Norfolk), each of whom inherited about £100,000 as his co-heiresses. MP for Maldon, 1741–7.

EAST WALL:

62 *William Brownlow* (1699–1726)
Sir GODFREY KNELLER (1646/9–1723)
Younger brother of Viscount Tyrconnel. Died impoverished by the collapse of the South Sea Bubble, when his brother put up a fulsomely worded monument to him in Belton church. Painted, like his sister's portrait (No. 144, West Staircase), and for her, in 1719.

63 *Elinor Dewe, Mrs Pepper*
Sir GODFREY KNELLER (1646/9–1723)
Signed and dated 1680
Sister of Mrs Richard Sherard and aunt to Alice, Lady Brownlow, in whose education she assisted. She became the second wife of Dr Robert Pepper (d.1700), Chancellor of the Diocese of Norwich.

WEST WALL:

64 *? Elizabeth Cust, Mrs John Cockayne* (1649–1739)
BRIAN BIRDE
Signed: *Brianus Birdeus Pinxit: Anno: 86*
Only surviving daughter of the first Sir Richard Cust and Beatrice Pury, and sister of Sir Pury Cust. In 1670 she married John Cockayne (d.1719) of Cockayne Hatley, Bedfordshire, which, after the death of their only surviving son Samuel in 1745, passed successively to cadet members of the Cust family, who incorporated the name Cockayne into their own. Pendant of No. 2, Marble Hall.

65 *William Brownlow* (1699–1726)
ENOCH SEEMAN (c.1690–1745)
For biography, see No. 62.

66 *Sir John Sherard, Bt* (1662–1724)
JOHN RILEY (1646–91)
Brother-in-law of 'Young' Sir John. So addicted to a game of dice called 'Hazard' that he had to enter a bond of £2,000 with his brother-in-law not to play it.

67 *Beatrice Pury, Lady Cust* (1623–1715)
ENGLISH, mid-seventeenth-century
Heiress of the Purys of Kirton, married Sir Richard Cust, 1st Bt of Stamford (1622–1700) in 1644.

68 *Portrait of a Lady*
MICHAEL DAHL (1656?–1743)

FURNITURE

Italian rosewood and marquetry cabinet inlaid in tortoiseshell, late seventeenth-century.
English oyster-veneered laburnum-wood domed coffer on a stand, late seventeenth-century.
A set of six walnut and beechwood chairs and an armchair, all late seventeenth-century. They are in the style of Thomas Roberts, a furniture-maker to the royal palaces.
The bureau cabinet, veneered in burr-walnut, is roughly contemporary with the other furniture in the room, dating from around 1715. The doors of the cabinet retain their original engraved mirror plates, and open to reveal an elaborate interior with tiers of drawers and pilasters of *verre églomisé*, which are repeated in the lower section. Further panels of this rich form of decoration occur in the pediment.

CERAMICS

Most of the porcelain is either *famille verte* or Japanese Imari.

THE STAIRCASE HALL

The placing of the main staircase off-centre is the only structural feature to break the overall symmetry at Belton. The Staircase Hall, known as the Little Marble Hall until about 1830, formed part of the ceremonial route for important visitors to the house, linking the Marble Hall with the Great Dining Room (now the Library) on the floor above. It retains its two finest seventeenth-century features, the paved floor by William Stanton and the plasterwork ceiling by Edward Goudge.

STAIRCASE

The present staircase maintains Sir Jeffry Wyatville's decorative scheme, carried out between 1813 and 1823. The oak balusters replaced the originals of pear wood and were completed in 1823.

DECORATION

The Vitruvian scroll following the line of the stairs and the gold and white colours are Wyatville's and date from 1819. The wainscot was grained and the handrail varnished at the same period. The wainscot graining, which seems to have been painted out already by the time the 6th Lord Brownlow had the room redecorated in the 1960s by Francis Johnson, has recently been restored.

PLASTERWORK CEILING

This is by Edward Goudge, whose name appears in the account books in 1687. It incorporates the Brownlow crest of a greyhound on a cap of maintenance in the corner cartouches, bordered by scrolling sunflowers and a garland of fruit and flowers.

PICTURES

There were 43 pictures, 'all Gold Gilt frames, some being large' on the stairs, when the house was first furnished.

68A *John Hume (Egerton Cust), Viscount Alford*
(1812–51)
Sir FRANCIS GRANT, PRA (1803–78)
Eldest son of the 1st Earl Brownlow, who predeceased his father in 1851. By descent through his maternal grandmother he successfully claimed the vast Ashridge and Ellesmere estates on the death of the last Earl of Bridgewater in 1849.

ON STAIRS:

74 *Dorothy Mason, Lady Brownlow*
(1665?-99/1700)
Sir GODFREY KNELLER (1646/9–1723)
For biography see No. 25, Saloon.

99 *Sir William Brownlow, 4th Bt* (1665–1702)
Sir GODFREY KNELLER (1646/9–1723)
He inherited Belton after the death of his elder brother, 'Young' Sir John, in 1697, but never lived here himself. He was the father of Viscount

Tyrconnel and of Anne Brownlow who, through marriage, brought Belton into the Cust family.

73 *Lady Adelaide Talbot, Countess Brownlow*
(1844/5–1917)
Sir FRANK O. SALISBURY, RA (1874–1962)
Signed
Daughter of the 18th Earl of Shrewsbury, married in 1868 to the 3rd Earl Brownlow. With no children, they devoted themselves to the restoration of Belton and its gardens. Painted in the boudoir of their other home, Ashridge Park. Exhibited RA, 1908.

69 *Adelbert Wellington Brownlow Cust, 3rd Earl Brownlow* (1844–1921)
Sir FRANK O. SALISBURY, RA (1874–1962)
The last Earl Brownlow, in his uniform as Lord Lieutenant of Lincolnshire and Honorary Colonel of the Lincolnshire Yeomanry. Exhibited RA, 1908.

77 *Lady Adelaide Talbot, Countess Brownlow*
(1844/5–1917)
FREDERICK, LORD LEIGHTON, PRA (1830–96)
For biography, see No. 73. Later described by Lady Paget as the 'most beautiful of three sisters, every one of them the salt of the earth', she was one of the older generation of the group of aesthetically minded aristocrats known as 'the Souls' (see p. 33). This is perhaps the finest of Leighton's female portraits. The autumnal landscape was painted at Ashridge. Exhibited RA, 1879.

SCULPTURE

An officer in seventeenth-century costume, bronze, by Sir Joseph Edgar Boehm, RA (1834–90), 1866.

The 3rd Earl Brownlow (1844–1921) and his horse 'Queen Bess', bronze, by Sir Joseph Edgar Boehm, RA (1834–90), 1871.

Sophia Hume (1787/8–1814), first wife of the future 1st Earl Brownlow, by Joseph Nollekens, RA (1737–1823), 1815.

George III (1738–1820), by Sir Richard Westmacott, RA (1775–1856).

FURNITURE

Speaker Cust's leather-covered robe chest, on a contemporary mahogany stand.
A late seventeenth-century or early eighteenth-century Japanese lacquer coffer, mounted on a Rococo giltwood stand, c.1740.

The Staircase Hall before recent redecoration

A pair of eighteenth-century starting cannon.
A set of four hall chairs in the style of Wyatt. Renovated.
Giltwood side table in mid-eighteenth-century style.
Ormolu chandelier, 1830s, acquired from the Lansdowne House sale in 1931.

CERAMICS

A pair of Japanese Imari jars.

THE YELLOW BEDROOM

This is another of James Wyatt's surviving interiors. Originally called the White Painted Room, Lord Tyrconnel refurnished it in green and white. By 1754 the abundance of needlework upholstery gave it an added femininity. Wyatt did away with the four side windows, and opened the view of the park to the south through the present window arrangement. The room probably became known as the Yellow Bedroom in Wyatt's time.

DECORATION

Wyatt's decoration dates from 1777–8. Drawings show details for the cornice frieze, which was to have been matched in the upper part of the door entablature. The present door is probably Victorian and shows nothing of the earlier scheme. Wyatt also designed the overmantel mirror.

PICTURES

TO LEFT OF DOOR:

78 *Portrait of ?Henry Lapostre* (1672–1749)
Attributed to BALTHASAR DENNER (1685–1749)
On copper
Probably identifiable with a portrait of a '*Monsieur L'Apotre*' by Denner in Sir Abraham Hume's collection, for which the sitter's family had paid 50 guineas – five times the going rate. Lapostre was a rich Huguenot, without any known connection with the Humes. Denner worked in England in 1721–7.

79 *Supposed portrait of Sir Pury Cust, Kt* (1655–98/9)
Manner of JOHN VANDERBANK (1694?–1739)
Actually painted *c.*1730, when Sir Pury was long dead.

80 *Lady Anne Egerton, Duchess of Bedford* (d.1762)
Follower of Sir GODFREY KNELLER (1646/9–1723)
Only daughter of Scroope, 1st Duke of Bridgewater; shown here as the widow of her first husband, Wriothesley, 3rd Duke of Bedford (1708–32); in 1733 she married William, 3rd Earl of Jersey (d.1769).

EAST WALL:

81 *Sir Brownlow Cust, 1st Lord Brownlow* (1744–1807)
FRANCIS COTES, RA (1726–70)
For biography, see No. 15, Marble Hall. Painted in so-called 'Van Dyck' dress, and, according to Elizabeth Cust, uncompleted because of the painter's death.

82 *The Hon. William Cust* (1787–1845)
The Hon. ELIZABETH CUST (1776–1858)
Signed with initials
Painted here by his eldest sister in the dress of a Salt Bearer at the Eton Montem of 1805. Subsequently a barrister and Commissioner of the Customs.

83 *Eleanor Brownlow, Viscountess Tyrconnel* (1691–1730)
CHARLES JERVAS (*c.*1675–1739)
For biography, see No. 18, Tapestry Room. Probably painted a little before the same artist portrayed her husband in 1725 (No. 51, Tyrconnel Room).

84 *? Amelia Egerton, Lady Hume* (1751–1809)
Attributed to RICHARD COSWAY, RA (1742–1821)
For biography, see No. 9, Marble Hall. Possibly cut down from Cosway's *Portrait of Lady Amelia Hume with a Book*, recorded in her husband's collection.

WEST WALL:

85 *John William Spencer, 2nd Earl Brownlow* (1842–67)
Sir FRANCIS GRANT, PRA (1803–78)
Eldest son of Viscount Alford and Lady Marian Compton; succeeded his grandfather as Earl Brownlow in 1853. Died unmarried at Menton. This portrait was painted to celebrate his coming-of-age, in 1863.

86 *Pastoral Scene*
ENGLISH
Early nineteenth-century watercolour

87 *Classical landscape with travellers and a river*
GASPAR DE WITTE (1624–81)
Signed lower right
From Viscount Tyrconnel's collection.

88 *View of Greenwich*
ROBERT GRIFFIER (1688–c.1750)
Signed bottom mid-left: *R. GRIFFIER F./1729*
From the collection of Viscount Tyrconnel, who took a house at Greenwich for a change of air when his first wife fell ill in 1729. The Griffiers seem to have specialised in painting Greenwich from different viewpoints; here the half-completed Hospital, and Wren's Royal Observatory, on the far left, are visible.

89 *Lady Marian Compton, Viscountess Alford*
(1817–88)
Sir FRANCIS GRANT, PRA (1803–78)
Eldest daughter of 2nd Marquess of Northampton, she married John, Viscount Alford, in 1841. Brought up in Italy by a liberal father, she became an accomplished artist and friend of artists, designer of Alford House, Prince's Gate, a historian of needlework, and founder of the Royal School of (Art) Needlework. Painted in 1841, and exhibited at the RA in 1842.

90 *Pastoral Scene*
ENGLISH
Early nineteenth-century watercolour

ABOVE THE DOOR:

91 *Dr Richard Cust* (1728–83)
G. ALLEN
Dated 1762
Youngest son of Sir Richard Cust and Anne Brownlow (cf. No. 140, West Staircase); Rector of Belton in 1770. No painter called G. Allen is known, so the later inscription may be wrong. Elizabeth Cust says that it was 'by a bad painter at Bath; considered a strong likeness'.

BED

Regency mahogany four-poster bed with giltwood ornaments and cornice, with cream-coloured flossy silk couched work incorporating the monogram of Lady Marian Alford, mother of the 2nd and 3rd Earls. The piece was made up into a bed in 1927.

FURNITURE

Late eighteenth-century overmantel mirror.
Pair of Regency mahogany bedside cupboards with ormolu mounts.
An early Victorian giltwood cheval mirror.
Regency mahogany firescreen, with embroidered banner.
Pair of early eighteenth-century side chairs with seats embroidered in seventeenth-century manner.
Regency mahogany tea-caddy.
Giltwood prie-dieu, mid-Victorian.
Giltwood boudoir chair, early Victorian.
Regency mahogany sofa table and chest of drawers in the manner of Gillow & Co.
Regency mahogany washstand.
Giltwood pier-glass, mid-eighteenth-century design.

CLOCK

Empire-style black-and-white marble mantel clock.

PORCELAIN

Most notable in the room are the seven pieces of Sèvres porcelain of a very rare mirror-black ground colour, *c.*1780. The chinoiserie decoration is applied in gold and platinum.

THE CHINESE BEDROOM

The decoration of this room dates from *c.*1840, though the wallpaper is eighteenth-century. It is difficult to decide whether the room was fitted to the wallpaper or vice versa. Its proportions have been altered since the late seventeenth century, when it was known as 'the drawing roome next to the best Chamber': on the south side, a false wall has been erected, making a passage between the main staircase and the Chinese Bedroom and giving access to the Queen's Bedroom from the East Landing. The cornice, dado and other joinery are painted to imitate bamboo.

WALLPAPER

The Chinese wallpaper is decorated with a continuous scene of a garden party running around the lower part. The paper is made up of square hand-painted sections and in places some of the birds and butterflies were cut out and applied separately.

BED

The bed, which appears to date from *c.*1840, has a gilded and scrolled canopy and glazed chintz hangings and matching curtains. The coverlet is blue embroidered satin.

The Chinese Bedroom

FURNITURE

This room houses some of the collection of japanned wares included in the original furnishing of Belton.

Chinese lacquer coffer with engraved gilt-metal angles and lockplates, late seventeenth-century. Purchased at the Christie's sale with the help of Prof. and Mrs Anthony Mellows.

Two early eighteenth-century side chairs and ebonised dining chair.

A wing armchair.

George III lacquer side table.

Giltwood overmantel mirror.

Chinese ivory table cabinet and lacquer coffer.

Japanese lacquer table cabinet.

Chinese export lacquer table cabinet on bamboo-pattern stand.

Pair of white-painted and gilt scroll pelmets, *en suite* with the bed.

Japanese lacquer side table and matching armchair, nineteenth-century.

CARPETS

Aubusson carpet and hearth rug, nineteenth-century.

CERAMICS

ABOVE THE FIREPLACE:

Chinese *famille verte* porcelain.

Pair of Chinese *cloisonné* enamel quails, late eighteenth-century.

THE QUEEN'S BEDROOM

This room takes its name from Queen Adelaide, widow of William IV, for whose visit in September 1841 it was redecorated. Prior to that the room had changed its name at least four times, and had been used both as a bedroom and as a picture room. Centrally situated over the Saloon, it was originally known as the 'Best Chamber'.

DECORATION

The panelling, which is contemporary with the date of the building, was stripped in this century, in the time of the 6th Lord Brownlow. It has recently been redecorated to resemble its appearance at the time of Queen Adelaide's residence in the house. The furnishing also dates from this early Victorian redecoration.

CHIMNEY-PIECE

The marble chimney-piece is not original, but contemporary in design with the furniture. The D-fender is Victorian.

WOOD CARVING

The carved wood frieze panel above the fireplace may be one of those for which Edmund Carpenter was paid in 1688.

PICTURES

SOUTH WALL, OVER DOOR TO LIBRARY:

157 *Alice Brownlow, later Lady Guilford*
(1684–1727)
Manner of WILLIAM WISSING (1653–87)
Third daughter of 'Young' Sir John and Alice, Lady Brownlow; married in 1703 to Francis, 2nd Baron Guilford (1673–1729), as his second wife. Cf. No. 49 (Tyrconnel Room).

OVER MANTELPIECE:

123 *Elizabeth Brownlow, later Countess of Exeter*
(1681–1723)
WILLIAM WISSING (1653–87)

Eldest daughter of 'Young' Sir John and Alice, Lady Brownlow; married in 1699 to John, Lord Burghley, afterwards 6th Earl of Exeter, as his second wife.

WEST WALL, OVER DOOR TO ANTE-LIBRARY:

41 *Flowerpiece*
JEAN-BAPTISTE MONNOYER (1636–99)
A flowerpiece by Monnoyer is almost a *sine qua non* of old English collections.

EAST WALL, OVER DOOR TO CHINESE ROOM:

39 *Flowerpiece*
MARIO NUZZI, called MARIO DE' FIORI
(c.1603–73)
From Tyrconnel's collection; possibly the unascribed 'flower piece over ye Door' of the Damask Bed-Chamber in his London house.

BED

This is probably the canopy bed with a dome upholstered in 1813 by William Stephens, later refurbished in the revived Rococo style, with a parcel-gilt canopy and Queen Adelaide's monogram in silver embroidery on the headboard.

The Queen's Bedroom before recent redecoration

A Chinese powder-blue and gilt vase, K'ang Hsi period (1662–1722)

The crimson and ivory striped silk of which the hangings and the curtains are made and with which the chairs, the sofa and the pole-screens are uphol-stered has been re-woven recently to match the original moire-ed striped silk which had decayed to an irreparable state. The braids, fringes and tassels, however, are all original and have been carefully cleaned and repaired before being re-applied to the bed and the curtains.

Ivory satin bed coverlet, nineteenth-century.

FURNITURE

Pair of Regency mahogany bedside cupboards with ormolu mounts, which resemble published designs by Gillows.

Dutch marquetry *armoire*, the panels of flowers attributed to the seventeenth-century master Van Maekren.

Pair of stained beechwood and mahogany pole-screens, *c.*1840.

Mid-eighteenth-century giltwood pier-glass.

Victorian tub-shaped easy chair.

Early Victorian light oak sofa.

Regency rosewood table inlaid with brass, and rosewood book carrier.

TEXTILES

Aubusson carpet and hearth rug.

On either side of the room are two interesting panels of linen, printed to resemble tapestry, with flower baskets and vases among stringwork scrolls inhabited by birds.

CERAMICS

The powder-blue and gilt vases are Chinese of the K'ang Hsi period.

ON MANTELPIECE:

Japanese Imari vases mounted as lamps, early eighteenth-century.

THE ANTE-LIBRARY

Except for a short spell as a bedroom, until 1876 this was the dressing-room to the adjoining Morris Room (not shown to the public), although being next to the best bedchamber (now the Queen's Bedroom), it may also have been used by the occupants of that room: it probably served as Queen Adelaide's dressing-room during her visit in 1841. The 3rd Earl made it into an Ante-Library when the Library was fitted out in 1876 – the press-numbers survive around the tops of the cases – but more recently the room has been used as a china cabinet to display some of Belton's porcelain.

DECORATION

The bolection-moulded fireplace and overmantel are probably original to the room. The marbling seems to date from 1884, when W. & J. Scar-borough were paid for 'painting upper arched ceiling to Anti-Library 4 coats & marbling Dᵒ in different marbles & varnishing the same'.

CERAMICS

PLATES ON WALL: Chinese *famille rose* Qianlong, *c.*1750.

WHITE GODDESSES: *blanc-de-Chine* figures of Guan-yiz made at Dehua in southern China, late seventeenth-century and early eighteenth-century.

LARGE BOWL ON LACQUER CABINET: very fine Japanese Imari, late seventeenth-century.

INSIDE CABINET: All Japanese Imari, early eighteenth-century, except for the teapots and trencher salts, which are Chinese Imari, *c*.1725–50.

CHINA AROUND ARCHWAY: Mostly Chinese K'ang Hsi *famille verte*, late seventeenth-century and early eighteenth-century.

TWO SQUARE VASES (SECOND SHELF LEFT): Japanese, late seventeenth-century.

SQUARE WHITE VASES: Chinese Qianlong, late eighteenth-century.

TALL VASE: Chinese *famille verte*, nineteenth-century.

BOWL (TOP LEFT): Chinese Imari, early eighteenth-century.

CABINET TO LEFT: Mostly Japanese Imari, early eighteenth-century, except for the large bowl on the top shelf, the ewer, two teapots, two dishes and the plate on the second shelf and the dish on the third shelf, which are all Chinese Imari, early eighteenth-century.

CABINET FACING: All the white pieces are Dehua, *blanc-de-Chine*, late seventeenth-century and early eighteenth-century, except for the vases on the bottom shelf, which are late eighteenth-century and are not *blanc-de-Chine*. The remainder are *famille rose* Qianlong, 1740–60.

CABINET TO RIGHT: Blue-and-white service with the arms of Sir Richard Cust and his wife Anne Brownlow in *famille rose* enamels, *c*.1730. Blue-and-white service with the arms of Viscount Tyrconnel, *c*.1730.

THE LIBRARY

This room has twice been transformed since the seventeenth century, when it was the Great Dining Room. In 1778 James Wyatt changed it into a classical drawing-room with a shallow vaulted ceiling in delicate plasterwork, and swept away all traces of its original Caroline decoration. In 1876 the 3rd Earl converted it into a library.

DECORATION

Drawings survive in Wyatt's hand for the ceiling and various elevations. His intention was to paint the ceiling in a scheme of pale pinks and greens; and

The Library chimney-piece incorporates the figures of Pomona and Ceres, the Roman goddesses of fruit and of the earth; attributed to Sir Richard Westmacott

the lunettes and roundels of the ceiling were to have been filled with mythological scenes, rather than the putti pictures by Elizabeth and Lucy Cust at either end of the room. However, it seems unlikely that any part of this decorative scheme was carried out. The plasterer is not specifically named in surviving bills, but may well have been the otherwise unknown Utterton, who was paid £67 7s for decorating the adjoining Boudoir in 1777, and received a further £63 for unspecified work two years later.

CHIMNEY-PIECE

The marble chimney-piece has caryatid supports representing Ceres and Pomona (the Roman goddesses of the earth and of fruit) and a bacchic frieze. Attributed to Sir Richard Westmacott, RA, it was not part of Wyatt's scheme for the room, which had a more delicate chimney-piece with columns supporting an overmantel mirror extending the whole height of the wall.

PICTURE

39A *John Cust, 2nd Baron and 1st Earl Brownlow* (1779–1853)
Sir MARTIN ARCHER SHEE, PRA (1769–1850)
Signed and dated 1835
John Cust succeeded his father as 2nd Baron Brownlow in 1807. He was elevated to an earldom in 1815. He commissioned Sir Jeffry Wyatville's work in the house and gardens at Belton. He is painted here in his uniform as Lord Lieutenant of the county and bearing the Hanoverian badge of the Royal Guelphic Order.

SCULPTURE

Venus de' Medici and *The Belvedere Antoninus*, both eighteenth-century Florentine bronzes after classical originals.

Bronze model of the *Machine Gun Corps Memorial*, by Gilbert Bayes (1872–1953). The Corps was raised at Belton; during the First World War the park became a small tented town with railway tracks and training grounds for the artificers and engineers.

BOOKCASES

These were designed for Sir Jeffry Wyatville, perhaps by his cousin Edward Wyatt, and made in 1809, originally for what are now the Hondecoeter and Breakfast Rooms. They were installed in the Library by the Grantham firm of John Hall in 1876.

FURNITURE

English desk, *c.*1760, missing its original leather top. Several pieces of library furniture which correspond with early nineteenth-century designs from Gillow & Co. of Lancaster: traditional library reading chair with book rest, metamorphic chair that turns over to form library steps, green leather armchairs by the fireplace, and mahogany folio cabinets.
The exercise chair or 'library horse' sadly, is unlikely to be that made for Lord Tyrconnel in 1754 (the year of his death) by his own joiner, Samuel Smith, who was paid £2 19s 2d 'for a new Chamber Horse

Vigorous bouncing on exercise chairs such as this was thought to be good for the health. Viscount Tyrconnel bought himself a 'chamber horse' in 1754, the year of his death. Sadly this 'chamber horse' is unlikely to be the one for which he paid £2 19s 2d in that year, as it appears, stylistically, to date from the early nineteenth century

which my Lord bespoke himself', as it would appear to date stylistically from fifty years later.

Pair of early nineteenth-century library globes made by W. & J. M. Bardin.

Speaker Cust's despatch boxes rest on contemporary mahogany stands. They were offered to Winston Churchill for use in Parliament, when the House of Commons was bombed in 1941.

The silver-bound casket contains an illuminated address presented to the 1st Earl on his retirement as Lord Lieutenant of Lincolnshire.

CLOCK

Ebonised bracket clock by John Johnson, seventeenth-century.

CERAMICS

ON CHIMNEY-PIECE:

Pair of tall Chinese *famille verte* and powder-blue vases, K'ang Hsi period.

Toby jugs of George V and Sir Winston Churchill.

THE BOUDOIR

This was originally furnished as a bedroom. The 1688 inventory describes its bed as having 'Gold Gilt Cupps & feete, wth Curtayns & Vallens of Staynd Silke, lind wth pinke collerd Silke'. In 1776–7 the room was entirely remodelled by James Wyatt as Lady Brownlow's dressing-room. Some of Wyatt's design remains, in particular the ceiling and cornice frieze, but since then it has been used as both a sitting-room and a bedroom. The 3rd Earl had the panels and large overmantel installed in the 1870s. The room was redecorated in 1963 as a boudoir.

DECORATION

The plasterwork ceiling has been repainted as it was originally conceived. The plasterer may have been Utterton (see the Library above). Wyatt's elevations show the walls a plain colour, probably the 'Green Flock Palm Paper' bought from a Mr Stark in 1777. The 3rd Earl's panels were originally filled with green striped damask; these panels, together with the appliqué drops of acanthus husks, a new chimney-piece with paired columns at either side and an oval overmantel mirror, were produced by George Jackson & Sons. In the 1960s the decayed

damask was replaced by Francis Johnson with wall hangings of flock paper.

CHIMNEY-PIECE

The chimney-piece was replaced in the 6th Lord Brownlow's time by one more in keeping with the room, with inset copper plaques in the manner of Angelica Kauffmann, representing Juno, Minerva and Apollo. Though not included among Wyatt's surviving designs, this may be the original chimney-piece, which must have been the work of William Tyler (d.1810), who had executed monuments in Belton church to Speaker Cust and his wife.

PICTURES

ON THE EASEL:

186 *Portrait of a Lady*
Manner of JOHN SINGER SARGENT (1856–1925)
A portrait in *profil perdu* that never fails to intrigue visitors, yet the identities of both sitter and artist are unknown. It may have been some connection with Harry Cust, although the 5th Lord Brownlow is said to have seen it in the window of a Bond Street gallery, and to have been captivated by it.

WEST WALL:

100 ? *Thomas Revel*, MP (d.1752)
Attributed to WILLIAM HOARE of BATH (1706–99)
Pastel
To all appearances, the husband of No.125, of Fetcham, Surrey; but subsequently confused with the sitter in No.78, Yellow Bedroom.

101 *Jane Egerton, Mrs Revel*
Attributed to WILLIAM HOARE of BATH, RA (1706–99)
Pastel
One of the daughters of Captain the Hon. William Egerton (cf. No.141, West Staircase); married No.100 in 1738.

102 *Frances Pembrook, Lady Bankes* (1728–1806)
WILLIAM HOARE of BATH, RA (1706–99)
Pastel
Daughter of Charles Pembrook, married to Henry Bankes (No.106) in 1754. By contrast with (the earlier) Nos 100 and 101, in Hoare's more elaborate Rococo type of frame.

Wyatt's Neo-classical plasterwork ceiling was put up in the Boudoir in 1776–7

NORTH WALL:

103 *Jane Cust, Mrs James Evelyn* (1725–91)
THOMAS HUDSON (1701–79)
Second daughter of Sir Richard Cust and Anne Brownlow. This picture and its pendant (No. 104) were paid for in 1756.

104 *Lucy (Cockayne) Cust* (1732–1804)
THOMAS HUDSON (1701–79)
Fourth daughter of Sir Richard Cust and Anne Brownlow, and longest surviving of the whole family. Added the name of Cockayne on succeeding her brother Francis (d.1791) at Cockayne Hatley. Pendant to No. 103.

105 *Children acting as Macbeth and the Witches*
JOHN WESTBROOKE CHANDLER
(1762–1807)
Sketch for a larger picture exhibited at the RA in 1787 as: 'Portraits of four daughters of a gentleman at play, as Macbeth and the witches'. Not necessarily, as once thought, the daughers of Lord Brownlow, who would have been called a 'nobleman'.

EAST WALL:

106 *Sir Henry Bankes* (1711–74)
WILLIAM HOARE OF BATH, RA (1706–99)
Pastel
Father-in-law of 1st Baron Brownlow, and one of

the formers of the picture collection at Belton. Grocer, Sheriff of London and knighted 1762.

107 *Dorothy Cust* (1729–70)
Attributed to THOMAS HUDSON (1701–79)
Third daughter of Sir Richard Cust and Anne Brownlow. Probably painted a little before Hudson's half-lengths (Nos 103 and 104), at the same time as No. 108.

108 *Etheldred, Lady Cust* (1720–75) *and her son, Brownlow* (1744–1807)
Attributed to THOMAS HUDSON (1701–79)
Daughter and co-heiress of Thomas Payne of nearby Hough-on-the-Hill, Lincolnshire, and Elizabeth Folkes; married Sir John Cust in 1743. Mother of the 1st Baron Brownlow, seen here before he was breeched.

109 *Elizabeth Cust* (1724–69)
Attributed to ENOCH SEEMAN (c.1690–1745)
Eldest daughter of Sir Richard Cust and Anne Brownlow. The painter of this charmingly naive portrait has shown the spaniel chasing a bluebottle!

FURNITURE

Mahogany silver table in the Chinese Chippendale style.
Chinese lacquer cabinet with copper mounts on a mid-seventeenth-century giltwood stand, with a nineteenth-century Regency ormolu gallery rail added on three sides.
A large overmantel mirror in the style of Wyatt, made in 1875.
George III giltwood pier-glass, introduced by Wyatt.
Louis XVI rosewood and bois clair trellis and dot parquetry *bureau plat*.
North Italian giltwood side chairs, nineteenth-century.
Regency circular table, the top of which is inlaid with coloured marbles.

CARPET

Aubusson tapestry carpet, c.1900. Although Wyatt offered two alternative designs for a carpet for this room, both of which mirrored the ceiling, there is no evidence that either was ever woven.

PORCELAIN

Two uncoloured Bow porcelain figures, c.1750–2. They represent Henry Woodward and Kitty Clive,

popular actors of the day, in costume as the 'Fine Gentleman' and the 'Fine Lady' in David Garrick's first play, *Lethe*, which was produced in 1740.
Meissen Marcolini coffee set in green and gold stripes, late eighteenth-century.

THE WINDSOR BEDROOM

Named in honour of Belton's association with Edward VIII, although the present Prince of Wales, while a cadet at RAF Cranwell, was the most frequent visitor to use the room in recent times. It was last decorated for the 6th Lord Brownlow's third wife, Leila.

PICTURES

EAST WALL:

110 *Sophia Hume, Lady Brownlow* (1787/8–1814)
?JOHN RISING (1753–1817)
Younger daughter of Sir Abraham Hume (No. 8, Marble Hall) and first wife of the future 1st Earl Brownlow (No. 126); commemorated by Canova's monument in Belton church.

111 *Lady Adelaide Talbot, Countess Brownlow* (1844/5–1917)
'E. M.' or 'M.E.', 1885
For biography, see No. 73, Staircase Hall.

112 *The Children of the Rev. Henry Cockayne Cust*
ENGLISH, *c*.1823
The children are, from left to right: Anna Maria (1817–36), Henry Francis (1819–84), Lucy (1818–44), Eleanor (later Mrs Walter Seton-Kerr, 1823–1903) and Robert (1821–1909).

113 *Amelia Hume, Lady Farnborough* (1772–1837)
Manner of JOHN HOPPNER, RA (1758–1810)
Elder daughter and co-heiress of Sir Abraham Hume (cf.No. 8, Marble Hall) and Amelia Egerton, and thus sister-in-law of the 1st Earl Brownlow. A celebrated amateur watercolourist.

114 *Lady Adelaide Talbot, Countess Brownlow* (1844/5–1917)
EDWARD CLIFFORD (1844–1907)
Pastel
The model for the relief by Lady Feodora Gleichen on her monument in Belton church. For biography, see No. 73, Staircase Hall.

SOUTH WALL:

115 *Portrait of a young girl in yellow*
Manner of Sir GODFREY KNELLER (1646/9–1723)
This and No. 116 were probably cut out of a larger portrait or portraits.

116 *Portrait of a young girl with a rose*
Manner of Sir GODFREY KNELLER (1646/9–1723)

117 *Violet Manners, Duchess of Rutland* (1856–1937)
NINA CUST (1867–1955)
Pencil drawing. Monogrammed NW
The greatest beauty of the 'Souls' (cf. No. 77, Staircase Hall) and herself a sensitive artist, primarily of portrait drawings; she also designed a moving memorial to her elder son, who died aged nine, for the chapel at Haddon Hall in Derbyshire. Nina Cust (cf. No. 122) became her protégée.

WEST WALL:

118 *Angel with grapes*
LOUISA, MARCHIONESS OF WATERFORD (1818–91)
Pencil and watercolour
Another aristocratic amateur artist, known for her distinctive watercolours, very often of children. (She had none herself.) Her major work was the decoration of Ford School in Northumberland with biblical murals. Ruskin said, 'She might have been a Paolo Veronese had she been poor.'

119 *Katherine Kinloch, Lady Brownlow* (d.1952)
OLIVE SNELL (fl.1910–40)
Black chalk and watercolour
Inscribed: *To Lord Brownlow from Olive Snell, 1929*
Presumably the portrait that the 6th Lord Brownlow mentioned in a letter to his aunt, Nina Cust, in March 1929: 'I had a rather lovely watercolour sketch done of Kitty while on the boat by a woman called Olive Snell, who, although rather hackneyed in her work, has produced something I think quite likeable.' For biography, see No. 131.

120 *Angel with an apple and a candle*
LOUISA, MARCHIONESS OF WATERFORD (1818–91)
Pencil and watercolour
Pendant to No. 118.

121 *Peregrine Cust, 6th Baron Brownlow* (1899–1978)
CUTHBERT ORDE (1888-?)
Charcoal drawing. Signed: *ORDE 1942*
Son of the 5th Baron and Maud Buckle. Close friend of Edward VIII, later Duke of Windsor, and

Lord-in-Waiting during his brief reign. Responsible, with his second wife, Dorothy, for much of the repair and redecoration of Belton in the 1960s.

NORTH WALL:

122 *Emmeline Welby-Gregory, Mrs Henry Cust* (1867–1955)
Manner of the Hon. JOHN COLLIER, RA (1850–1934)
Better known as Nina Cust, daughter of Sir William Welby-Gregory, 4th Bt, of Denton, Lincolnshire. Draughtswoman, sculptress and author. Her husband Harry Cust (1861–1917), whom she married in 1893, was a hardened womaniser, who froze her out of his life and the circle of the 'Souls'. In spite of this she remained devoted to him, carving his tomb in Belton church and keeping a copy of the effigy in her drawing-room.

122A *The Hon. Sir Edward Cust and the Hon. Lady Middleton*
THE HON. ELIZABETH CUST
The artist was the daughter of Brownlow Cust, 1st Baron Brownlow. She was responsible for drawing up a critical catalogue of paintings at Belton in the early nineteenth century, including her own works which, with characteristic modesty, she placed in the final section entitled 'Artists Unknown'.

PICTURES ABOVE MANTELPIECE:

124 *Anne Mason, Countess of Macclesfield, later Mrs Brett* (1666?–1753)
THOMAS FORSTER (c.1677–after 1713)
Graphite on vellum. Signed and dated 1704(?)
For biography, see No. 46, Tyrconnel Room.

125 *Unknown mother and child*
Photograph

126 *The Hon. John Cust, later 1st Earl Brownlow* (1779–1853)
Silhouette, dated 1801
Eldest son of 1st Baron Brownlow and Frances Bankes, created 1st Earl Brownlow in 1815. A classical scholar. His first wife was Sophia Hume (No. 110), through whom the Bridgewater estates came to the family.

127 *The Hon. and Rev. Henry Cockayne Cust* (1780–1861)
Silhouette, dated 1832
For biography, see No. 11, Marble Hall.

128 *Sir Brownlow Cust, 1st Baron Brownlow* (1744–1807)
Silhouette, 1801?
For biography, see No. 15, Marble Hall.

129 *Young girl holding a rose*
Photograph

130 *Anne Brownlow, later Lady Cust* (1694–1779)
THOMAS FORSTER (c.1677–after 1713)
Graphite on vellum. Signed and dated 1704
For biography, see No. 144, West Staircase.

131 ? *Katherine Kinloch, Lady Brownlow, as a girl* (d.1952)
Monogrammed 'L. de C.'(?)
Younger daughter of Brigadier-General Sir David Kinloch, Bt, married 6th Baron Brownlow in 1927. Mother of the present Baron Brownlow.

132 ? *Francis Cockayne Cust, KC, MP* (1722–91)
JOHN DOWNMAN, ARA (c.1750–1824)
Watercolour
The legal robes suggest this may be Sir Richard Cust's third son, as Recorder of Boston (from 1760) or Treasurer of the Middle Temple (from 1784).

FURNITURE

Regency cheval mahogany mirror.
Pair of armchairs.
Pair of mid-eighteenth-century mahogany side chairs.
Late eighteenth-century giltwood and composition cheval firescreen with a tapestry banner.
Laburnum and ebony secretaire, c.1830.
Mid-eighteenth-century mahogany serpentine dressing chest and basin stand.
Late eighteenth-century mahogany press.

CERAMICS

A collection of Sèvres cups, saucers, plates and other European porcelain.

THE WINDSOR CORRIDOR

PICTURE

133 *The Library at Chancellor's House*
FLORENCE SETH
The Custs lived in a seventeenth-century house in Hyde Park Gate (now demolished) and 'Nina's decor made it seem like a house in the country' (Abdy & Gere, *The Souls*, p. 81).

View of Belton; by an unknown English artist, c.1720. This shows the south front enclosed by a wrought-iron screen (now gone), the West Courtyard to the left, and the church beyond. The outsize figure of the porter is holding the staff which now hangs beside the painting

THE WEST STAIRCASE

Known in the late seventeenth century simply as the 'Staircase by the Dining Room Door', this was originally a service stair. It was probably altered by Wyatville, c.1810, and acquired a new importance from the late nineteenth century when the 3rd Earl turned the West Entrance into the family entrance, and began the habit of using the west side of the house as the family's living quarters.

PICTURES

UPPER LANDING:

134 *Sir Richard Brownlow, 2nd Bt* (1628–68)
Attributed to HENRY ANDERTON (c.1630–70)
Eldest surviving son of Sir William Brownlow of Great Humby; married Elizabeth Freke (No. 44, Tyrconnel Room) in 1652; father of 'Young' Sir John and Sir William Brownlow. Lived at Ringston Hall, given him by 'Old' Sir John. Not by Lely, as inscribed.

135 *View of Belton*
ENGLISH, c.1720
This shows the south front of the house enclosed by a wrought-iron screen with stone piers, which were replaced by Lord Tyrconnel with a curved *clair-voyée*. Also visible are the West Courtyard, as it was

prior to the building of the range that closed its north side in the late nineteenth century, and the church beyond. The outsize figure of the porter, probably Henry Jewel, holds the staff which now hangs beside the picture.

136 *Lady Sophia Bentinck, Duchess of Kent* (d.1748)
HERMAN VAN DER MYN (1684–1741)
Signed and dated 1731
Introduced to Belton by the 1st Earl Brownlow, whose first wife, Sophia Hume, was the Duchess's great-granddaughter. The sitter was daughter of the 1st Earl of Portland, and the second wife of Henry Grey, Duke of Kent (m.1728/9).

137 *Portrait of an Unknown Young Woman*
ENGLISH, c.1650

138 *Dorothy Mason, Lady Brownlow*
(1665?–99/1700)
MICHAEL DAHL (1656–1743)
For biography, see No. 25, Saloon.

139 *Sir Richard Cust, 2nd Bt* (1680–1734) *as a boy*
ENGLISH, c.1690
Son of Sir Pury Cust by his first wife, Ursula Woodcock; married the future heiress of Belton, Anne Brownlow, in 1717; father of Speaker Cust, and of the whole progeny painted after his death in No. 140.

WEST ENTRANCE HALL:

140 *The Cust Family*
ENOCH SEEMAN (*c*.1690–1745)
The greatest might-have-been of Belton: Hogarth was originally approached to paint this immense family-piece of the widowed Anne Brownlow, Lady Cust, and her children in 1741, but his price was too high. It was Seeman's last and largest picture. Those represented are, from left to right: Francis Cockayne Cust, MP, KC (1722–91); Captain William Cust, RN (1720–48), pointing at a map of a naval engagement; Jane Cust, subsequently Mrs Fane, then Mrs Evelyn (1725–91); Peregrine Cust, MP, DCL (1723–85); Savile Cockayne Cust (1698–1772), Sir Richard's half-brother; Rev. Richard Cust, DD (1728–83); Sir John Cust, 3rd Bt, Speaker of the House of Commons (1718–70); Anne Brownlow, Lady Cust (1694–1779); Lucy Cockayne Cust (1732–1804); Elizabeth Cust (1724–69); Dorothy Cust (1729–70). Sir John holds a miniature of his new wife, Etheldred Payne (1720–75), and a portrait of a (deceased?) boy hangs on the wall.

141 ? *Capt. the Hon. William Egerton*, MP (1684–1732)
CHARLES JERVAS (*c*.1675–1739)
Fourth son of the 3rd Earl of Bridgewater, whose second son, Henry, Bishop of Hereford, was grandfather of Amelia, Lady Hume (No. 9, Marble Hall). If the inscription identifies the sitter correctly, the date of 1734 must be wrong, as Egerton was dead by then.

142 *Thomas Payne* (1687–1742)
ENGLISH, *c*.1720
Father of Etheldred, the wife of Speaker Cust.

LOWER WEST STAIRCASE:

143 *Portrait of an unknown young Gentleman*
ENGLISH, late seventeenth-century

144 *Anne Brownlow, Lady Cust* (1694–1779)
Sir GODFREY KNELLER (1646–1723)
Signed and dated 1719
Daughter and eventual heiress of Sir William and Dorothy, Lady Brownlow, and sister of Viscount Tyrconnel; married Sir Richard Cust in 1717. 45 years a widow, she devoted herself to her large family (No. 140). Inheriting Belton in 1754, she made over her own house in Grantham (also N T) to her son, Sir John, but exchanged with him again in 1766, so that he should have a house befitting his dignity as Speaker.

145 ? *John Cockayne* (1641–1719)
ENGLISH, mid-seventeenth-century
When Sir Richard Cust, 1st Bt, of Stamford, gave his eldest daughter Elizabeth to be married to this John Cockayne in 1670, he gave her the then handsome fortune of £2,500, in consideration of which her husband settled the Cockayne Hatley estate in Bedfordshire on her and her issue. The estate ultimately passed to the Rev. Henry Cockayne Cust, through whom this and other Cockayne portraits came to Belton.

146 *Chief Justice Sir Thomas Jones* (*c*.1612–1692)
After WOLFGANG WILLIAM CLARET (fl. London *c*.1665–1706)
The sitter became Chief Justice of the Common Pleas in 1683, but was dismissed in 1686 in a clash with James II's attempts to achieve royal supremacy. There is some uncertainty as to why the portrait should be at Belton. The association of Claret with the Egerton family provides the only clue.

147 *Portrait of a boy*
ENGLISH, mid-seventeenth-century
Just possibly the otherwise untraced 'picture of Sir John Brownlow (when a child)' recorded in the Best Wrought Bedroom in 1754.

SCULPTURE

Harry Cust (1861–1917), by his wife Nina Cust (1867–1955).
Marble
For biographies, see No. 122, Windsor Bedroom.

FURNITURE

Two late seventeenth-century walnut and gilt pier-glasses.
A coromandel incised lacquer chest.

THE ANTE-ROOM

In Lord Tyrconnel's day the Ante-Room was the 'Little Room by the Library'. The 1737 inventory shows that its contents included two chairs (one of which was a 'black leather bottomed chair on wheels'), 34 prints, and a 'map of Belton'. Today it is a sitting area for visitors, and contains newspaper cuttings and other items charting the course of the Abdication and old photographs of the house.

PICTURES

EAST WALL, STARTING AT THE TOP AND GOING DOWN EACH ROW:

148 *Portrait of a Gentleman*
FRANZ HALS

149 *A Tavern Interior*
Attributed to CORNELIS DUSART (1660–1704)
Ascribed to Cornelis Dusart when given to the collection by the widow of Dr Richard Cust, and certainly typical of his imitations of his master, Adriaen van Ostade.

150 *Church Interior*
HENDRIK VAN STEENWICK the Elder (c.1550–1603)
The only survivor at Belton of four such church interiors in Tyrconnel's London house in 1754. The figures may be by another hand.

151 *A hermit at his devotions*
Imitation of GERARD DOU (1613–75)
On panel
Bought by Sir Henry Bankes from a picture-dealer at Antwerp called Pilaes in 1754, with the surprising appreciation that: 'The hands are a little too large, but the Head is as fine as painting can be.' The resemblance to Dou is minimal.

152 *Christ and the Woman of Samaria*
BOLOGNESE, early seventeenth-century
From Viscount Tyrconnel's collection.

153 *A river landscape*
Sir ABRAHAM HUME, Bt (1749–1838)
Signed and dated 1824 on the back of panel
A good example of the collector as artist (see No. 8, Marble Hall).

154 *Dorothy Mason, Lady Brownlow*
(1665?–99/1700)
WILLIAM WISSING (1653–87) and JOHN VAN DER VAART (1653–1727)
Signed by both artists, and dated 1687
For biography, see No. 25, Saloon.

SOUTH WALL:

170A *'La vie champêtre'*
FRANÇOIS BOUCHER (1703–70)
An early work, painted in a Dutch style. From the collection of Sir Henry Bankes and recently returned to Belton as a bequest from Mrs Martha Sklarz.

156 *Lord and Lady Tyrconnel in the park at Belton*
PHILIPPE MERCIER (1689–1760)
Mercier's masterpiece, and the outstanding picture at Belton. The participants would appear to be, from left to right: Viscount Tyrconnel (wearing the red sash of the Bath); the artist; Mrs Dayrell (Lady Tyrconnel's cousin), in the swing; Viscountess Tyrconnel (already perhaps something of an invalid), being wheeled by a blackamoor page; Francis Dayrell, looking at his wife; Savile Cust, pulling the string; William Brownlow (cf. No. 62, Blue Bedroom), Lord Tyrconnel's brother, looking outward. The south front of Belton appears in the background. Painted in 1724–6.

36 *Madonna and Child*
Attributed to FRA BARTOLOMEO (1472–1517)
The most distinguished survival from the collection of Sir Abraham Hume, who bought it in Florence in 1787. Berenson may have been right in thinking it by Fra Bartolomeo himself. It is strongly influenced by Raphael's late Florentine Madonnas.

WEST WALL:

158 *St William of Aquitaine taking the habit*
After GUERCINO (1591–1666)
Bought by Sir Abraham Hume at Bologna in 1786, in the belief that it was Guercino's own study for the celebrated altarpiece in S. Gregorio (now Pinacoteca Nazionale, Bologna).

159 *Jan van de Wouwer, or 'Waverius'*
(1574–1636)
Attributed to Sir ANTHONY VAN DYCK (1599–1641)
On panel
Financial Counsellor to the Governor of the Spanish Netherlands, and a friend of Rubens. Bought by Sir Henry Bankes in 1754 as a Van Dyck, but not certainly by him. It relates more closely to Van Dyck's bust-format etching for his *Iconography*, than to the half-length portrait in the Pushkin Museum, Moscow.

160 *The infant Bacchus with the Nymphs of Nysa*
Manner of ANDREA SCHIAVONE (1522–63)
On panel
From Viscount Tyrconnel's collection. Jupiter's son by Semele was brought up in secrecy by the Nymphs of Nysa, to conceal him from the jealousy of Jupiter's wife, Juno.

NORTH WALL, STARTING AT THE TOP AND GOING DOWN EACH ROW:

161 *The Madonna of the Rabbit*
After CORREGGIO (*c.*1489/94–1534)
One of the most copied of all Correggio's compositions (the original is now in Capodimonte); named after the rabbit half in the picture at the left. Also known as *La Zingarella* ('The Gypsy Woman') because of the Virgin's headgear.

162 *Birth of the Virgin*
GIUSEPPE CHIARI (1654–1727)
Pendant of No. 168, and also adapted from a picture painted for the Cappella Marcaccioni.

163 *A Nymph and a Satyr*
ABRAHAM GOVAERTS (1589–1626)
From the collection of Sir Henry Bankes, who paid 16 guineas for it in 1754. May represent Jupiter in the guise of a satyr about to seduce Antiope.

164 *The Madonna*
Manner of CARLO MARATTA (1625–1713)
From Sir Henry Bankes's collection, and still in his good English Rococo frame.

165 *The Penitent Magdalene*
TITIAN (*c.*1485–1576)

166 *Dead Christ mourned by angels*
After GUERCINO (1591–1666)
Bought by the 1st Earl Brownlow in 1810 from a Mr Ruyssen, 'an eminent instructor in Oil Painting', who perhaps made this copy. The original is now in the National Gallery, London.

167 *Hagar and Ishmael*
SOPHIA HUME, LADY BROWNLOW (1787/8–1814)
after P. F. MOLA (1612–66)
Signed and dated 1809 on reverse
Sophia Hume evidently inherited her father Abraham's interest in Old Masters and ability to copy them (cf. No. 153). Probably copied from a picture in her father's collection, sold in 1923 and now in the Suida-Manning collection in New York.

168 *The Adoration of the Magi*
GIUSEPPE CHIARI (1654–1727)
This picture and its pendant (No. 162) are two of the few original Old Masters of any quality to survive at Belton, in this case from Tyrconnel's collection. It is an adaptation of Chiari's earliest major commission, the altarpiece of the Cappella Marcaccioni in S. Maria del Suffragio in Rome (*c.*1682).

169 *The Rest on the flight into Egypt*
Attributed to JAN BRUEGHEL II (1601–78)
and PEETER VAN AVONT (1600–52)
Panel
One of a group of pictures bought by Sir Henry Bankes from a Mr van Laucher in Antwerp in 1754. Ostensibly a Madonna and Child in a landscape, but St Joseph can just be discerned watering the ass in the distance.

OVER THE DOOR LEADING INTO THE HALL:

170 *Margaret Brownlow* (1687–1710)
MICHAEL DAHL (1656?–1743)
For biography, see No. 19, Tapestry Room.

THE TAPESTRY ROOM

This room was redecorated by Wyatville in 1811–12. Nothing survives of Francis Bernasconi's ceiling and cornice decoration from the same period. The room was remodelled *c.*1890 by the 3rd Earl Brownlow in convincing seventeenth-century style: Bernasconi's plasterwork was removed, new panelling in oak was provided for the walls and George Jackson & Sons put up the pastiche plaster ceiling. The same company probably also supplied the limewood carvings above the chimney-piece.

Before 1890 it had served as a dining-room (in the seventeenth century) and a common parlour (in the eighteenth century); the 3rd Earl wanted a setting for the *Diogenes* tapestries. The carpet is turkey pile.

FIREPLACE

All that survives from the Wyatville period is the fireplace. It was originally placed centrally on the east wall, according to Wyatville's drawing, which also shows that a picture of William III (who visited Belton in October 1695) was to hang above it. The coal box and D-fender are Regency.

TAPESTRIES

These date from the early eighteenth century and are said to have been found in the attics, where they were being used as carpets. They illustrate scenes from the story of Diogenes, inspired by the etchings of, or engravings after, Salvator Rosa, and were probably made at the Mortlake factory south-west of London. The borders, incorporating the arms of Viscount Tyrconnel, are of a slightly later date. The

The Tapestry Room

tapestries are: *Alexander visiting Diogenes in his tub; Diogenes writing on the lintel above the door of the cave; Diogenes breaking the cup*; and *The School of Plato*. The larger pair is listed in the 1754 inventory as hanging in what is now the Red Drawing Room.

PICTURES

17 *Portrait of an Unknown Woman*
Attributed to Sir GODFREY KNELLER
(1646/9–1723)
Impossibly inscribed as Elizabeth Freke, wife of Sir Richard Brownlow, 2nd Bt, who would have been in widow's weeds by around 1680, when this portrait would have been painted.

18 *Eleanor Brownlow, later Viscountess Tyrconnel*
(1691–1730)
JOHN BAPTIST CLOSTERMAN (fl.1690–d.1713)
Youngest and prettiest of the four married daughters of 'Young' Sir John Brownlow and Alice Sherard. In 1712 she was married to her cousin, later created Viscount Tyrconnel (No.51, Tyrconnel Room). Evidently painted by the younger and inferior of the Closterman brothers.

OVER DOOR TO MARBLE HALL:

19 *Margaret Brownlow* (1687–1710)
Sir GODFREY KNELLER (1646/9–1723)
Third daughter of 'Young' Sir John Brownlow. In 1710 his widow tried to arrange a marriage to Lord Sherard, but Margaret declared that she would rather die first. Lord Willoughby then presented himself, and she did die (of smallpox).

FURNITURE

Louis XV kingwood commode, stamped twice by the maître ébéniste François Mondon (1694–1770).
Gilt gesso pier-glass, *c.*1700.
Blüthner boudoir grand piano.
Set of four early eighteenth-century side chairs.
Early eighteenth-century giltwood side table with cover of eighteenth-century silver-thread flowered brocade.
Mahogany stool, *c.*1770.
Regency penwork games box.
Amboyna-wood cigar box.
Indian rectangular ivory box.
Louis XIV scarlet Boulle *bureau Mazarin.*

CLOCK

Louis XV Boulle bracket clock. The case dates from c.1750, with a later movement by Vulliamy, c.1850, numbered '1397'.

CERAMICS

Pair of Regency ormolu candelabra in Sèvres porcelain vases, an ormolu-mounted *famille verte* hexagonal bottle vase, a *famille rose* rouleau vase, a garniture of lobed hexagonal K'ang Hsi blue-and-white vases, and a small Chinese vase. The K'ang Hsi garniture is arranged in the traditional manner on the fireplace overmantel.

THE STUDY

Like so many of the rooms at Belton, the Study has changed its name several times over the last three centuries. Known in 1688 as the 'Corner Chamber by the Dineing Room', it soon became 'the School Room', presumably forming part of a suite of rooms for 'Young' Sir John Brownlow's daughters, whose nurseries were directly above. By 1737 it was Viscount Tyrconnel's library, and it has remained essentially a male preserve ever since.

PICTURES

OVERDOOR:

155 *Sir Pury Cust, Kt* (1655–98/9)
ENGLISH, late seventeenth-century
For biography, see No. 16, Marble Hall.

IN ALCOVE:

Madonna and Child
Attributed to PIER FRANCESCO FIORENTINO, ITALIAN, fifteenth century

THE BREAKFAST ROOM

This room was until recently used as a private dining-room. In 1809–10 Wyatville drew up plans for a 'Great Library' (now the Hondecoeter Room) and 'Ante Library' (the Breakfast Room) for the 1st Earl Brownlow. Both rooms were fitted with bookcases now in the 3rd Earl's Library upstairs. The walls were finished with a gilt plaster cornice and fluted band around the ceiling. The architect originally intended that a narrow door fitted with

sham books should connect this room with the Red Drawing Room, but this was rejected in favour of double doors in the centre of the west wall. The Egyptian-style marble fireplace also dates from the Wyatville period.

PICTURES

Nos 26–32 in the Red Drawing Room are best viewed from this room.

OVER FIREPLACE:

171 *The Hon. John Cust, later 1st Earl Brownlow* (1779–1853) (on the right), and the Hon. Henry Cust (1780–1861)
JOHN HOPPNER, RA (1758–1810)
For the sitters, see No. 126, Windsor Bedroom, and No. 11, Marble Hall. Painted in 1795.

172 *Maud Buckle, Lady Brownlow* (d. 1936)
Sir FRANK O. SALISBURY, RA (1874–1962)
Signed
Daughter of Captain S. Buckle, RE; married Adelbert Cust, who at that time had no especial prospect of succeeding to the title and lived at Cockfosters, in 1895. Pendant to No. 187.

173 *Prospect of Belton*
J. F. NOLLEKENS, 'Old Nollekens' (1702–48)
Signed and dated
This is one of three views of Belton, all of which were in Lord Tyrconnel's collection according to Elizabeth Cust, and all of which are today in this room. It shows Tyrconnel's extensive re-laying out of the grounds, as recorded by Badeslade, at the time of the building of Belmount Tower (1749–51). The attribution to 'Old Nollekens', despite the signature, is uncertain because of the likely date, which is rather too late for a painting by this artist in this style. J. F. Nollekens was the father of the celebrated sculptor, Joseph Nollekens.

BETWEEN THE WINDOWS:

174 *The Hon. and Rev. Henry Cockayne Cust* (1780–1861)
ENGLISH, nineteenth-century
For biography, see No. 11, Marble Hall.

175 *Major Henry Francis Cockayne Cust* (1819–84)
STEPHEN CATTERSON SMITH (1806–72)
Eldest son of No. 174; major in the Shropshire Yeomanry, captain in the 8th Hussars and MP for Grantham. Father of Harry Cust and the 5th Baron Brownlow.

176 *The Hondecoeter Room at Belton*
EDMUND FAIRFAX-LUCY (b.1945)
Commissioned by the Foundation for Art.

NORTH WALL:

177 *Frances Bankes, Lady Brownlow* (1757–1847)
*with her son, the Hon. John Cust, later 1st Earl
Brownlow* (1779–1853)
GEORGE ROMNEY (1734–1802)
Signed and dated 1783
Sittings for this portrait are recorded between
March 1783 and June 1784; it cost 60 guineas. Lady
Brownlow was the only daughter and heiress of the
collector Sir Henry Bankes. Married to the future
1st Baron Brownlow in 1775 as his second wife, she
bore him eleven children.

178 *The Park at Belton*
Attributed to PHILIPPE MERCIER (1689–1760)
This may be the 'Prospect of Belton by Mercier'
listed at Tyrconnel's Arlington Street house in 1738.
It shows the park and garden more or less as
engraved in *Vitruvius Britannicus* (1717). It is not by a
professional view-painter, since numerous inac-
curacies show that it was not done on the spot. No
other view-painting by Mercier is recorded, and it
lacks the sophisticated ease of the (later?) Brownlow
conversation piece (No.156, Ante-room). None the
less, the figures do suggest an artist influenced by
Watteau, as the young Mercier certainly was,
though the landscape is probably by another, less
capable hand.

76 *John William Spencer, 2nd Earl Brownlow*
(1842–67)
GEORGE FREDERICK WATTS, RA, OM (1817–1904)
For biography, see No.85, Yellow Bedroom.

180 *Sir Brownlow Cust, 1st Baron Brownlow*
(1744–1807)
GEORGE ROMNEY (1734–1802)
Painted four years before the Romney of his wife
and eldest son (No.177); sittings are recorded
between May and June 1779, and the portrait cost 36
guineas. For biography, see No.15, Marble Hall.

181 *The Cascade at Belton*
? THOMAS SMITH OF DERBY (fl. 1743–67)
The Cascade was created in 1745, and Viscount
Tyrconnel must have had it painted by Smith of
Derby soon afterwards; the picture was recorded in
the Chapel Drawing Room after his death, but
seems to have been removed by his widow; this
painting may not be the original. He also had the

picture engraved by Vivares in 1749, and had
framed prints sent to all his relatives.

EAST WALL:

182 *Katherine Kinloch, Lady Brownlow* (d.1952)
SIMON ELWES, RA (1902–75)
Signed and dated 1939
For biography, see No.131, Windsor Bedroom.
Shown standing in the park at Belton.

183 *Emmeline ('Nina') Welby-Gregory, Mrs Henry
Cust* (1867–1955)
The Hon. JOHN COLLIER, RA (1850–1934)
Signed on the reverse
For biography, see No.122, Windsor Bedroom.

184 *Edward John Peregrine Cust, 7th Baron Brownlow*
(b.1936)
HOWARD MORGAN (b.1949)
Signed bottom right: *MORGAN XI.88*
Lord Brownlow gave Belton House, some of its
contents and the garden to the National Trust in
1983. Autograph replica of the portrait commissioned by the Foundation for Art in 1986 for
presentation to Lord Brownlow.

185 *Peregrine Adelbert Cust, 6th Baron Brownlow*
(1899–1978)
EDWARD I. HALLIDAY (b.1902)
Signed and dated 1956
For biography, see No.121, Windsor Bedroom.
Shown standing on the roof of Belton, with Bel-
mount Tower in the background.

179 *Adelbert Wellington Brownlow Cust, 3rd Earl
Brownlow* (1844–1921)
GEORGE FREDERICK WATTS, RA, OM (1817–1904)
Signed
For biography, see No.69, Staircase Hall.

OVER DOOR TO WEST STAIRCASE:

187 *Adelbert Salusbury Cockayne Cust, 5th Baron
Brownlow* (1867–1927)
Sir FRANK O. SALISBURY, RA (1874–1962)
Signed and dated 1925
Son of Henry Francis Cockayne Cust (No.175) and
Sarah Cookson, Adelbert succeeded to the title of
Baron Brownlow on the death of his namesake, the
3rd and last Earl, in 1921. Salisbury was an im-
mensely successful painter, whose early portraits (eg
Nos 69 and 73, Staircase Hall) show a feeling for
pattern and drama, but who later simply held a
mirror up to the rich and powerful.

Edward John Peregrine Cust, 7th Lord Brownlow by Howard Morgan (No. 184; Breakfast Room)

FURNITURE

Mahogany breakfast table, *c*.1820.
Five mid-eighteenth-century mahogany dining chairs.
Pair of frosted glass wine coolers used as table lamps.
Pair of Regency mahogany serving tables, in the style of the cabinet-maker Thomas Hope.
Regency D-fender.

CERAMICS

In the display cabinet is a collection of English porcelain from the Chelsea and Derby factories, including dishes in the shape of cabbage-leaves and sunflowers, mid-eighteenth-century.

TEXTILES

Feraghan carpet.

CLOCK

Regency clock, by Vulliamy.

THE RED DRAWING ROOM

The 1698 inventory describes this as the 'white varnished drawing room', and it was later known simply as the North Drawing Room. In 1810 the room was redecorated by Wyatville and it retains much of its early nineteenth-century appearance.

DECORATION

Wyatville replaced a single door with double doors to connect with the Breakfast Room, then part of his newly created suite of library and ante-library. He also added draped curtains and reeded poles, and had his painter George Hutchinson gild the cornice and frieze. The original wall panels of rose du Barry crimson silk, hung by Gillow & Co. (which also provided much of the furniture), were replaced by paper of a similar pattern and colour in 1963. The carpet is Aubusson, *c*.1830.

PICTURES

The paintings in this room, hung in tiers as in the early nineteenth century, together with some of those in the Ante-room, are all that remain today of a once much larger collection of subject pictures.

EAST WALL:

27 *A Wooded Landscape with a Fountain*
ITALO-FLEMISH, eighteenth-century

28 *The Holy Family with the Infant St John the Baptist*
CARLO MARATTA (1625–1713)

29 *Laundresses washing clothes at a fountain*
The Hon. ELIZABETH CUST (1776?–1858) after
JAN MIEL, IL BAMBOCCIO (1599–1663)
Signed and dated (on back) 1802
This daughter of the 1st Lord Brownlow not only compiled a scholarly catalogue of the pictures at Belton, but was also an accomplished painter in oils.

30 *Italianate Landscape*
Manner of SALVATOR ROSA (1615–73)
Tyrconnel collection.

31 *The Rest on the Flight into Egypt*
GIUSEPPE CHIARI (1654–1727)

32 *A Shepherd Boy with sheep*
PETER PAUL ROOS called ROSA DA TIVOLI
(1657–1706)
From Tyrconnel's collection. Elizabeth Cust believed that this was the picture that Roos is reputed

to have painted for a bet during a round of cards, in less than half an hour.

SOUTH WALL:

33 *Portrait of a Jew*
Attributed to SALOMON KONINCK (1609–56)
From the collection of Sir Abraham Hume (see p. 38). Quite possibly an autonomous work by Salomon Koninck, on which the false Rembrandt signature and date of 1632 were put later.

34 *Shipping Scene*
Imitator of WILLIAM VAN DE VELDE the Younger (1633–1707)
Despite the supposed signature and date of 1696 on a spar bottom left, this appears to be a native imitation of the works that the Van de Veldes produced after they settled in England in 1672–3.

35 *Mary Hill, Lady Killigrew*
After Sir ANTHONY VAN DYCK (1599–1641)
A partial copy of the figure of Lady Killigrew in the double portrait by Van Dyck at Wilton House in

Wiltshire. Mary Hill was the wife of the courtier and playwright Sir William Killigrew (1606–95).

OVER CHIMNEY-PIECE:

96 *Queen Henrietta Maria, wife of Charles I*
UKNOWN ARTIST

37 *Presentation of the Virgin*
After TITIAN (c.1485–1576)
A reduced copy of the large picture in the Accademia in Venice. From the collection of Sir Abraham Hume, who thought it Titian's sketch for this. Hume wrote one of the earliest serious studies of Titian (1829).

WEST WALL:

26 *Madonna and Child*
After GUIDO RENI (1575–1642)
A detail copied from an often repeated *Flight into Egypt* by Reni. From Viscount Tyrconnel's collection, according to Elizabeth Cust.

40 *Shipping in an Estuary*
Manner of CHARLES BROOKING (1723–59)

38 *The Penitent Magdalen*
CARLO CIGNANI (1628–1719)
From Tyrconnel's collection in Arlington Street. Cignani and his pupil Franceschini, represented the last flowering of Bolognese Classicism.

ON THE BUREAU PLAT:

42 *An unknown Earl*
Attributed to J. L. SANDERS (1750–1825)
Miniature

43 *A Lady*
Attributed to JAMES SCOVELL (fl.1815–40)
Miniature

FURNITURE

Regency giltwood sofa, possibly supplied by Gillows in 1810.
Sabre-leg armchairs of the same date, in the style of the furniture makers Marsh & Tatham.
Regency pier-glass.
Late eighteenth-century giltwood sofa.
Late eighteenth-century semicircular side table with a marquetry top. There is a sketch drawing for this table in the archives.
Venetian giltwood torchères.
Pair of giltwood wall brackets.

A late seventeenth-century Italian lapis lazuli cabinet on a Charles II giltwood stand

Pair of nineteenth-century French ormolu firedogs, with figures of Nymphs after Nicolas Coustou.

Eighteenth-century kingwood *bureau plat* in the style of Charles Cressent (1685–1758), stamped.

Lapis lazuli cabinet of architectural form, Italian, late seventeenth-century. The Charles II giltwood stand is thought not to be the original, which may now be supporting the lacquered coffer (see below). The use of such a quantity of lapis lazuli, which is set in panels bordered with ebonised and parcel-gilt mouldings, is extremely rare; with its magnificent gilt stand carved with putti, acanthus branches and garlands of flowers, this is one of the most extravagant pieces of furniture at Belton.

Seventeenth-century coffer of speckled lacquer with sharkskin and mother-of-pearl inlay and silver mounts. The white-painted and parcel-gilt stand of about 1730 may originally have been made for the lapis lazuli cabinet in this room.

CLOCK

The case of the French ormolu clock is *c.*1790; the movement and dial are *c.*1810.

CERAMICS

The porcelain is mostly Chinese *famille rose*, mid-eighteenth-century, but the pair of blue mounted vases on the side table are Sèvres.

THE HONDECOETER ROOM

The early architectural history of this room is unclear, although it is possible that the kitchen in the west wing was originally of two storeys. If this were so, the Hondecoeter Room would originally have formed the upper part of that kitchen. From the early nineteenth century the room's history is easier to follow. In 1808 the Cambridge architect Charles Humfrey was called in to carry out preliminary structural work, and in the following year Wyatville installed the 1st Earl Brownlow's library here. In 1876 the bookcases were removed upstairs, and the 3rd Earl introduced neo-Caroline panelling with moulded garlands, perhaps by W. G. Rogers, creating a state dining-room as a fitting setting for the vast canvases by Melchior d'Hondecoeter which give the room its name. The present decoration revives that of the early twentieth century (after advice from Sir Edwin Lutyens), which had been degraded by successive repaintings.

FIREPLACE

This was brought from Ashridge Park and installed here after Lutyens had been consulted about the room.

Regency basket grate.

PICTURES

MELCHIOR D'HONDECOETER (1636–95)

188 *Open landscape with Poultry and Water-Fowl*

189 *View of a Park with Swans and Ducks*

190 *View of a Terrace, with a Page descending Steps*

All three are signed

Hondecoeter's major surviving set of decorative paintings. We do not know where in the Low Countries these scenes were originally painted for – or even if No. 188 originally belonged with Nos 189 and 190. Even before coming to Belton in 1873, they had been cut and adapted to fit another house in England. A fourth canvas (pendant to No. 188) could not be fitted in, and after various peregrinations (including a spell at Ashridge) is now in America. The paintings were restored between 1985 and 1990 at the Hamilton Kerr Institute.

OVER FIREPLACE:

191 *Dead Swan and Peacock*

JAN WEENIX the Younger (1642–1719)

Signed and dated 1708

Not part of the original scheme with the Hondecoeters, but complementing them perfectly. The younger Weenix was a cousin of Hondecoeter and specialised in such large and decorative game-pieces.

FURNITURE

Early nineteenth-century mahogany dining table.

Pair of late Georgian mahogany drop-leaf dining tables.

Pair of giltwood console tables.

Pair of late nineteenth-century silver lamp bases inscribed with texts celebrating the silver wedding anniversary of the 3rd Earl and Countess Brownlow in 1893.

Giltwood cheval screen with tapestry panel.

Twelve mahogany dining chairs, *c.*1830.

TEXTILES

Feraghan carpet.

View of a Park with Swans and Ducks; by Melchior d'Hondecoeter (No. 189, Hondecoeter Room)

SILVER

SILVER

Set of four two-light candelabra, by Paul Storr, marked for the year 1811.

THE NEW PLATE ROOM

This room was formerly the Serving Room. Built by the 3rd Earl in 1876 to provide direct access from the new state dining-room to the kitchens, it is now used to display some of the remarkable collection of Brownlow and Cust family silver (see Chapter Five).

PICTURE

192 *Prize beast*
JOHN E. FERNLEY (1782–1860)
This beast won the punch bowl on display in Cabinet 6, at the Smithfield Show in 1831.

THE FLOWER ROOM

The large nineteenth-century Minton dinner service on display is decorated with the Brownlow crest.

Visitors now go down to the Old Kitchen.

THE OLD KITCHEN

Kitchens were created in this high chamber in 1808–10 to replace those in the north wing of the house, which were destroyed when Wyatville's Library and Ante-Library were built for the 1st Earl Brownlow. Before the construction of the north range of courtyard buildings, these new kitchens were connected to the main house by a tunnel under the West Courtyard. The steps leading down to the tunnel can still be seen. The tunnel was equipped with trolleys run on wall-mounted tracks to convey the food to the house.

In 1876, when the Library moved to the first floor and the Hondecoeter and Breakfast Rooms took on their present appearance and function, the North Courtyard buildings were constructed to provide further access between the kitchen and the new state dining-room. During the twentieth century the kitchen returned to the basement of the house and this room was abandoned.

The room today is a compilation of what remains of the early nineteenth-century kitchen (the table, cupboards, hatch and some of the utensils), and recently constructed evocations of what may have existed (the range and decoration).

Of particular note is the set of fine monogrammed brass weights in their fitted box.

The visitor leaves the house to enter the West Court.

THE GATE SCREEN

The magnificent Baroque gate screen opposite is one of three early eighteenth-century wrought-iron screens at Belton. It is attributed to John Warren, who provided a similar screen for Denham Place in Buckinghamshire (designed by William Stanton, who supervised the construction of Belton) in 1692.

THE STABLES

Although contemporary with the house, the stable block is noticeably less sophisticated and suggests an architect with less flair than William Winde. It is almost certainly the work of William Stanton.

The north end of the Stables contained twelve stalls on the east side, presumably for carriage horses; another six of a more rustic nature on the west side, which were possibly used for heavy horses; and eight loose boxes for riding horses. The tea-room now occupies some of the stalls and the four-bay coach-house which formed the southern end of the block. A large staff of grooms and coachmen lived above the stables, and straw, hay and other feed were also stored there. The hoist used for lifting them is still in the roof.

THE BREWHOUSE

Across the entrance to the yard is the Brewhouse – designed by Jeffry Wyatville in the early nineteenth century, but substantially altered since his time – and a further three-bay coach-house. It now contains the shop and a display of carriages.

The little closed invalid carriage was built early in the present century for the 3rd Earl's wife, Lady Adelaide, who died in 1917. It was used to take the

The Stables

old lady for a sedate drive in the park, pulled by a pony and led by a groom.

The wooden sleigh is reputed to have been presented to the Brownlows by a Tsar of Russia in the nineteenth century. The reins passed between the two passengers to the driver, who occupied the little seat behind the body. The present Lord Brownlow's sister, the Hon. Mrs Partridge, is an enthusiastic horsewoman, and she had the invalid carriage restored and the sleigh painted in the 1960s, when the other two carriages in the Brewhouse were also acquired.

The late nineteenth-century spider phaeton was built by one of the finest London coach builders, Barker & Co. of Chandos Street. Phaetons were designed to be driven by the owner, and so the principal comfortable seat is at the front. Because of its size and weight, this particular example would probably have been drawn by one or two coach horses, rather than the smaller park horses more often used with this type of phaeton.

The other coach, a canoe-bodied or Sefton landau, was driven by a coachman. The easily raised and lowered hoods made it a versatile vehicle, suitable for all weathers. Built by Thorn of Norwich, its body is suspended on leather braces with twin perches and C-springs as well as elliptical springs – a type of double suspension normally used on rather grander carriages.

Next to the Brewhouse is the former indoor riding school, used by the family and their guests to ride in wet weather, and probably also for the schooling of horses. Its present roof was added during the Second World War.

CHAPTER SEVEN

THE GARDEN, CHURCH AND PARK

As with any major Caroline country house, Belton required an appropriately elaborate setting, and 'Young' Sir John Brownlow was already embarking on a dramatic transformation of the surrounding landscape as the first stone was being laid. In 1685 he planted no fewer than 21,400 ash trees and 9,500 oaks, along with 614 fruit trees, 260 limes, 2,000 roses and 100 gooseberry bushes. These new grounds may well have been laid out with advice from William Winde, who could also turn his hand to landscape design when the occasion demanded it: he later recalled how at Eastwell Park in Kent he had 'transplanted trees of a considerable bigeness wch did very well & the same I did at Sr Charles Kemishe orchard at Rupera in Wales [Ruperra Castle, Glamorgan]'.

The plan engraved by Hendrik Hulsbergh for Colen Campbell's *Vitruvius Britannicus* (1717) shows the results of 'Young' Sir John's endeavours, a highly developed scheme of formal parterres and walks to the north, south and east of the house. The main entrance to the south was approached through two courts: the first (F on Campbell's plan) had a circular drive that led into the second (G), a grid of paved walks crossing lawns ornamented with statues. To the south-east of this was a bowling green (E), while the north front looked out on to two elaborate parterres (B) bisected by a walk centred on an obelisk or fountain, and aligned with the main axis. Its boundary was marked then, as now, by the edge of the churchyard. To the west lay the kitchen garden (S) and orchards (V).

But the most dramatic scheme of all lay to the east. On the long axis of the house was the Great Pond (C), a canal constructed by John Holderness in 1685. This was flanked by close plantations shot through with symmetrical patterns of walks centred on *rond-points* in the style of the French garden designer André le Nôtre (1613–1700), whose for-malised arrangements of trees, water and planting had recently become highly fashionable in England. At the western end a small raised flower garden (D) gave access to the Chapel Drawing Room on the first floor of the house. Hulsbergh's engraving shows this surrounded by topiary trees, which also edged the *parterres de broderie* on the north side of the house. The garden and the park beyond were all enclosed by a five-mile wall in 1690.

Like so many of the spectacular baroque garden schemes of the later seventeenth century, 'Young' Sir John's formal landscape soon fell prey to changing tastes. His nephew, Viscount Tyrconnel, made a number of innovations, building a heated greenhouse – where melons were cultivated and experiments conducted to see if pineapples could be grown – and creating the Wilderness to the west of the house with its cascade and picturesque ruins, which still survive, although in a somewhat more ruinous state than when they were first conceived (see below). The appearance of the garden in Tyrconnel's time can be seen in three paintings (Nos 173, 178 and 181), which hang in the Breakfast Room, and in a bird's-eye view by Thomas Badeslade, made in the early 1750s.

Badeslade's engraving also shows what was the most significant departure from the seventeenth-century layout, the replacing of the Great Pond by a long walk. This came about by accident rather than design. In May 1751 a sluice which drained the Great Pond was inadvertently closed, with disastrous results, as Tyrconnel's nephew Peregrine reported:

The side of the great pond broke & in less than an hour the water run out intirely it broke down the Garden wall near the Statue of Cain & Abell, travers'd the Garden, broke down the wall that parts that & the Kitchen Garden went thro the latter, broke down the wall facing the Water just below Manton's Mill &

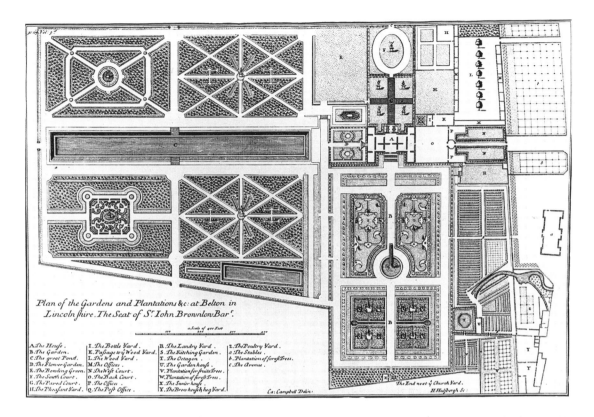

Plan of the Gardens and Plantations &c: at Belton in
Lincolnshire. The Seat of Sr. Iohn Brownlow Bart.

a Scale of 400 Feet

A. The House.
B. The Garden.
C. The great Pond.
D. The Flower Garden.
E. The Bowling Green.
F. The South Court.
G. The Paved Court.
H. The Pheasant Yard.

I. The Bottle Yard.
K. Passage to ye Wood Yard.
L. The Wood Yard.
M. The Offices.
N. The West Court.
O. The Back Court.
P. The Offices.
Q. The Post Office.

B. The Landry Yard.
S. The Kitching Garden.
T. The Octagon.
U. The Garden house.
V. Plantation for fruit Trees.
W. Plantation of forest Trees.
X. The Summer house.
Y. The Brewhouse & hog Yard.

z. The Poultry Yard.
a. The Stables.
b. Plantation of forest Trees.
c. The Avenue.

Ca: Campbell Delin:

The End next ye Church Yard.

H. Hulsbergh Sc:

(Above) 'Young'
Sir John Brownlow
surrounded his new
home with a highly
formal scheme of
parterres and walks;
engraving by Hendrik
Hulsbergh for Colen
Campbell's 'Vitruvius
Britannicus' (1717)

(Right) Prospect of
Belton; attributed to
J. F. Nollekens
(No. 173, Breakfast
Room). It shows
Tyrconnel's extensive
remodelling of the
grounds at the time
of the building of the
Belmount Tower
(1749–51) on the
horizon

there emptied itself; it ran with prodigious force & velocity & has done great mischief having destroyed the produce of the Kitchen garden such as Melons Pease &c & filled the whole space it ran over with sand.

As a result, the Pond was filled in, and, to quote Peregrine Cust again, Viscount Tyrconnel was 'unluckily deprived of one of the noblest sights in England'.

The next stage in the development of the Belton landscape was rather more considered. In 1775 the 1st Baron Brownlow's brother-in-law, Philip Yorke of Erddig, passed a pleasant afternoon riding over the estate, and dreaming of 'the Works which the present taste, and a Modern Improver, might raise about you', as he wrote to Brownlow. Those works would involve the extensive felling of trees to the south and east, including the whole of the South Avenue leading to the entrance front, part of the East Avenue, and all the close planting in the vicinity of the house.

Lord Brownlow evidently took Yorke's dreams seriously. Three years later, he engaged the landscape gardener William Emes (1729–1803) to draw up a 'Plan of the park and of the Demesne lands at Belton . . . with some Alterations'. Emes was employed at Erddig from 1767 to 1789, and it was presumably on Yorke's recommendation that Brownlow turned to him for advice on bringing Belton into line with 'the present taste'. In a development of Yorke's original scheme, Emes suggested an open pleasure ground surrounded by serpentine walks and woodland, and an Orangery to be built to the east of the house.

In the event, Emes's plans seem to have gone largely unexecuted, although the idea of a pleasure ground to the north of the house was approved, and the last of the parterres was removed to make way for it. In the east the formal seventeenth-century planting was thinned out to soften the rigid geometrical arrangements of the trees, so making the profile of the woods more naturalistic. This was, of course, in keeping with mid-Georgian fashions in landscaping, although there is a family tradition that Lord Brownlow did away with the formal garden because, in the 3rd Earl's words, he was 'terrified by the French revolution, and believing that it would spread to England gave up the amenities of life

saying that [it] was no use to maintain things that would soon be destroyed'.

Lord Brownlow's son, the 1st Earl, made further changes, with encouragement from his father-in-law Sir Abraham Hume, who, although chiefly remembered at Belton for his picture collection, was also a pioneering gardener. At Wormleybury, his Hertfordshire seat, he grew exotic paeonies and magnolias, developed a stove for warming tropical plants and was responsible for introducing Chinese chrysanthemums into Britain.

THE ITALIAN GARDEN

In 1810 the 1st Earl commissioned Jeffry Wyatville to redesign the area to the north-east of the house, which had until then been occupied by the kitchen garden. Wyatville's plans, submitted at intervals over a ten-year period, show an elegant classical landscape, with a large south-facing conservatory (now known as the Orangery) next to the church, a circular 'bason' with a fountain, and a dairy in the form of a small temple. The dairy was never built, and its place was eventually taken by Wyatville's Lion Exedra.

THE ORANGERY

The Orangery stands near the site of the pre-Brownlow manor house. Wyatville provided designs for the south elevation and for the internal layout, showing the positions of beds and the placement of two aviaries. Construction seems to have been delayed – perhaps by the death of the 1st Earl's wife Sophia in 1814 – but Wyatville was again at Belton in May 1819, and the small balusters on the roof were supplied by the Coade manufactory at Lambeth in 1819–20. The interior survives intact, with the exception of the roof, which was replaced in 1857 by a totally glazed version intended to introduce more light at a time when the cultivation of tropical plants was becoming fashionable. By 1890 a series of statues had been placed above the balustrade of the roof.

THE FOUNTAIN

Wyatville planned the fountain around 1810, although it was not built until 1816. The basin

(Above)   The Italian Garden, with the Orangery and Belton church in the background

(Right)   The Italian Garden in the late nineteenth century, showing the Repton-style pergola and elaborate box-edged parterres (both now gone) and the Lion Exedra

87

beneath was to be lined with pebbles in Roman cement, and, according to a pencil sketch dated 1821, a trellis of roses originally surrounded the fountain.

THE LION EXEDRA

This is also the work of Wyatville and dates from 1820. It was originally in the Dell on the west side of the Italian Garden, but was moved to its present position – the site proposed for the classical dairy – in 1921, replacing a garden seat at the end of an axial path.

The 3rd Earl Brownlow added box-edged parterres to what became known as the Italian Garden, and a cast-iron, ivy-covered pergola was placed around the fountain. The garden was edged with flowering shrubs, cherry, laburnum, may, viburnum, flowering currant, apple and pear. On either side of the Orangery were two parterres, one laid out as the Prince of Wales's feathers, and the other, to the west, as a series of small beds branching from a central vein. These were edged with box and planted with violas.

THE DUTCH GARDEN

The Dutch Garden is approached either from the north terrace, or via the garden door which opened from the wing built in 1877 to connect the north-

west corner of the house to the existing office block. Created in 1879, its layout was based on Hulsbergh's *Vitruvius Britannicus* engraving, and formed part of the 3rd Earl's neo-Caroline 'restoration' of Belton; it takes its name from the style of garden introduced to England from Holland in the late seventeenth century. Twenty-nine pieces of wrought stone were made in 1881 by Robert Lindley for steps leading down from the north terrace to the newly levelled site. Parterres lined the walk along the terrace, at either end of which were clipped box hedges and slatted wooden seats. There were originally 40 beds to each side of the central pathway, planted with aubrietia, arabis, grape hyacinth, phlox, primrose and auricula, while the stone cisterns were filled with tulips, violas and wallflowers. (The emphasis on spring blooms was due to the fact that the 3rd Earl and his wife rarely stayed at Belton during the summer months.) The golden and Irish yews were planted when the garden was laid out, as were the clipped yew hedges which neatly edge it.

GARDEN SCULPTURE AND ORNAMENTS

The central walk through the Dutch Garden leads to a limestone sundial in the form of Time with an attendant cherub. This was brought into the garden by Viscount Tyrconnel, and is by the Danish carver Caius Gabriel Cibber (1630–1700), 'sculptor in ordinary unto His Majesty' William III. The bronze dial itself is modern.

Beyond the sundial, at the far end of the main axis walk, is a figure of Ceres, dated 1850 and the work of the Italian sculptor Franchi. Four eighteenth-century life-size Italian marble figures, including Neptune, Flora and Venus, adorn the north terrace, along with two other statues – Pallas and Diana – which may be those listed in the 1754 inventory as having stood on the turf on the south front of the house. Some of the bewildering array of ornamental urns and vases must date from the Wyatville era, but others, including the massive rectangular cisterns, were introduced by the 3rd Earl in the late nineteenth century.

(Opposite) The Dutch Garden

During the First World War many of the Belton flower beds were turned over to the cultivation of fruit and vegetables, an enterprise which proved so successful that the 6th Lord Brownlow was able to say that 'the turnover of about £80 per month . . . is a model for an estate, although we only have four men'. The war effort also took the pergola from the fountain in the Italian Garden, as well as a box-and-yew maze which stood in the pleasure garden. In recent times the 6th Lord Brownlow's second wife, Dorothy, planted the borders of the Dutch Garden with scarlet roses, while his third wife, Leila, preferred pink and white tea roses. The present Lady Brownlow replaced them with yellow and white roses and borders of lavender.

BELTON CHURCH

The parish church of SS Peter and Paul (which is not the property of the National Trust) has always been closely associated with the owners of Belton, and still contains a remarkable group of Brownlow and Cust monuments.

In spite of major restorations, evidence of the Norman building still survives, including the north arcade, with its massive central pier decorated with incised lozenges, and the lower part of the west tower. The Perpendicular windows and the ceilings at the western end of the aisle are late medieval, while the upper tower bears the date 1638, the year in which it was rebuilt by Sir Richard Brownlow.

Virtually all of the rest of the church belongs to the nineteenth century. In 1816 the 1st Earl commissioned Jeffry Wyatville to design the chapel on the north side as a memorial to his first wife, Sophia Hume, who had died two years earlier. Wyatville's scheme drew heavily on the vocabulary of the existing late medieval work, embellishing it with convincing fan-vaulting and tabernacles in the angles of the north wall (although it proved a somewhat awkward setting for Canova's massive statue of *Religion*). The architect also refaced the whole of the north wall, and probably added the door in the west side of the tower, the pinnacles above, and the crenellations on the tower along the parapet of the nave and chancel. Later nineteenth-century work included the little vestry off the north chancel chapel, the restoration of the interior and the renewal of many of the fittings. The pews were installed in 1891 by the 3rd Earl Brownlow.

STAINED GLASS

The glass is all nineteenth-century. The east window is filled with three miracles of the raising of the dead, designed in 1847 by Thomas Willement (1786–1871). Their subjects are: *The Raising of the Young Men*; *The Raising of Jairus's Daughter*; and *The Raising of Lazarus*. Willement may also have been responsible for the armorial window in the nave, which dates from 1823.

THE PARK

In November 1690 William III's Secretary of State, the 2nd Earl of Nottingham, ordered the Solicitor General to prepare a Bill granting 'Young' Sir John Brownlow the right to 'enclose and Impark such of his Lands in Belton Manthorpe and Londonthorpe ... as he shall think fitt & Convenient for y⁰ propertie not exceeding one Thousand Acers'. At the same time 'Young' Sir John was also given the right to keep deer – something which he had apparently already been doing since at least 1686.

The earliest surviving map of the Belton estates dates from the time of this imparkment, although it is not clear as to how much of the estate was actually enclosed. The map shows an area stretching from Peascliffe in the west to Ermine Street in the east. The great Eastern Avenue, which ran from the house along the same east–west axis as 'Young' Sir John's Great Pond, is clearly visible, and may well date from before Richard Brownlow's purchase of Belton in the early seventeenth century – there is evidence to suggest that the oldest trees were planted in *c*.1580.

The most dramatic architectural features of the park owed their origins not to 'Young' Sir John or his predecessors, but to Viscount Tyrconnel, who between 1742 and 1751 introduced a picturesque Wilderness, a Gothick ruin and Cascade, and a prospect tower from which to enjoy his improvements to the landscape of Belton.

THE CASCADE IN THE WILDERNESS

In *c*.1742 Tyrconnel decided to exploit the potential of the River Witham to the west of the house, planting its valley with trees and shrubs, and draining the stream to create a waterfall, which was embellished with a Gothick ruin. The resulting

The Cascade: 'Design'd and executed, as I think, in a taste superior to anything that I have seen'; engraving by Francis Vivares, 1749, after ? Thomas Smith of Derby (No. 181, Breakfast Room)

picturesque landscape – shown in a 1749 engraving by Francis Vivares – was described by Tyrconnel in a letter to his nephew and heir John Cust in April 1745: 'a grand Rustick arch finished with vast Rough Stones over ye Cascade of ye River, and two Huge Artificial Rocks on each side, Design'd and executed, as I think, in a taste superior to anything that I have seen.' Unfortunately the designer's identity remains a mystery.

In the course of the nineteenth century a small rustic summer-house (with a floor made from the knuckle-bones of deer) was built on the banks of the river, with a graceful cast-iron bridge leading to it, but both have since disappeared. During the Second World War the Wilderness was opened to the public and in 1976 an adventure playground was built, together with a miniature railway.

THE BELMOUNT TOWER

The Belmount Tower was built between 1749 and 1751 by the master mason William Grey and the master builder and joiner Samuel Smith. It consisted of a tall arch flanked by two lower arches, supporting a single room reached by a spiral staircase, with a painted iron cupola topped by a gilded star, and a wooden balustrade on a hipped roof.

The Tower had a dual function. It terminated the Eastern Avenue, providing a focus to the vista from the house; and it served as a prospect tower from which Viscount Tyrconnel could enjoy views over his park. As such it became quite famous: after a visit to Belton in 1757, Mrs Philip Lybbe Powis recorded that 'from a temple in the garden called Belle Mount you may see seven counties at once, a thing from one spot thought very remarkable'.

Near the Tower, on the south side of the avenue, there was a small plantation, Eleanor's Bower, named after Tyrconnel's first wife and created some time before the death in 1721 of her mother, Lady Alice Brownlow.

In the later eighteenth century Tyrconnel's great-nephew, the 1st Lord Brownlow, made further changes to the park, with encouragement from

Philip Yorke. Yorke advised him that 'Belmount . . . may be well clipped its two wings; they are the most offending members, and I think sh'd be cut off'. Brownlow apparently took his brother-in-law's advice, since the arches have vanished, and today the Tower is supported by rather ugly buttresses. He also set about establishing plantations on the south side of the park, and by 1784 he had moved the main approach to Belton from the South Avenue to a new public road to the east, connecting

The Belmount Tower: 'from a temple in the garden called Belle Mount you may see seven counties at once, a thing from one spot thought very remarkable'

with the village thoroughfare to the north of the house. Yorke's other ideas included felling the late seventeenth-century South Avenue, to make way for a large serpentine lake with a 'handsome stone bridge over it ... from whence a dressed Road for ceremony only will lead you with a gentle inclination to the great steps'. However, these proposals were not carried out.

By the time of the 1st Lord Brownlow's death in 1807, the park had almost acquired the form that it retains today. The Grantham–Lincoln road which now forms its western boundary was built in 1804, and the Five Gates Road from Barkston Heath to Londonthorpe was completed, giving access between Belton and Londonthorpe. The South Avenue eventually became a private road to the house, reserved for ceremonial occasions, while the general entrance was from Belton village.

There were still some changes to come, however. The 1st Earl rebuilt the Keeper's Lodge on the north side of the Old Wood (a large plantation in the centre of the park), renovated the Gothick ruins over the Cascade, and called in the architect Anthony Salvin to design several summer-houses in the arboreta on the estate. The Earl's final, poignant contribution to the landscape of the park was a memorial to his son and heir Viscount Alford.

BOATHOUSE, TAR LANE AND VILLA PONDS

There are two streams which drain Belton Park in an east–west direction, both eventually flowing into the Witham on the western side of the park. The northern stream had two dams built across it, making Boathouse and Tar Lane Ponds, while the southern stream drains into Villa Pond. By the early nineteenth century several exotic trees had been mixed in with broadleaved specimens, to create a series of arboreta. The National Trust has reopened the lakeside walk.

THE BOATHOUSE AND HERMITAGE

In 1821 Anthony Salvin was commissioned to design a Tudor Alpine boathouse on the pond to which it gave its name. It is not known when the building was completed, but in 1826 repairs were being done to the plasterwork and the roof was slated. In 1833 some Windsor chairs were bought to

furnish it and a boat, bought in 1831, was in place. Sadly, the Boathouse has fallen into disrepair, but the National Trust hopes to be able to restore it in the near future.

In 1821 Salvin also designed a summer-house, which became known as the Hermitage, to be built at Villa Pond. His design was for a miniature cottage of one room, complete with a fireplace. Outside was a covered balcony with twisted cast-iron balusters and a little oriel window. The only surviving record relating to the construction of this cottage is a bill for thatching the roof in 1829. It fell into disrepair in this century and finally collapsed when a yew fell on it about twenty years ago.

THE ALFORD MEMORIAL

Soon after the death in 1851 of the 1st Earl's son and heir, Viscount Alford, Richard Westmacott was commissioned to design a monumental pillar to be erected south of the grove of trees half-way between Towthorpe and the Old Wood (now in the golf course). The eight-feet high column, placed on a pedestal and surmounted by a vase garlanded with flowers, was completed in 1852. Its touching Latin inscription reads: 'Farewell my dearest son. Among these trees, once fortunate in aspect, offered in your name against a prayer, I, your unfortunate father, weeping, place this here.'

The 3rd Earl, who succeeded in 1867, planted specimen conifers in the Wilderness and Boathouse Plantation, and rhododendrons and yew walks in the latter. He also laid out the south side of the park as a golf course; this was seriously damaged during the First World War, when an army camp, served by a railway from Peascliffe to Belmount, was erected in the park.

Perhaps the most significant change to the park landscape since the 3rd Earl's death in 1921 was the felling of the South Avenue, which, having survived various proposals for its eradication, finally succumbed to Dutch Elm disease in the 1970s. The National Trust, assisted by the Kensington and Chelsea Association of Trust members, has recently embarked on a plan to replant the whole avenue with Turkey oaks.

THE BROWNLOW AND CUST FAMILIES

Richard Brownlow*† (1553–1638), Chief Prothonotary of the Common Pleas = Katherine, dau. of John Page of Harrow and Wembley

Alice*† (1604–76), dau. of Sir John Pulteney of Misterton = 'Old' Sir John (baptised Anthony) Brownlow*† (1594–1679), 1st Bt of Belton (d.s.p.)

Sir William Brownlow (1595–1666), 1st Bt of Great Humby = Elizabeth (1601–66), dau. of William Duncombe of Great Brickhill, or Simpson, Bucks.

Audrey

Mary

Elizabeth (c.1592–1658) = John Sherard (d.1660) of Lobthorpe

Sir Richard Cust (1622–1700) 1st Bt of Stamford = Beatrice Pury (1623–1715)

William Brownlow (1633–75) of Snarford

Sir Richard Brownlow*† (1628–68), 2nd Bt = Elizabeth* (1634–84), dau. of John Freke of Shroton

Richard Sherard of Lobthorpe (d.1668) = Margaret, dau. of Lumley Dewe and sister of Elinor Mrs Robert Peppe*

Mary* = Peter Whitcombe

Elizabeth

Sir John Sherard* (1662–1724)

Alice* (2) (1666/7–1712), dau. of William Savile of Newton, Lincs. = Sir Pury Cust* (1655–98/9) = (1) Ursula* (1659–83/4), dau. and heiress of Edward Woodcock of Newtimber, Sussex

Sir William Brownlow* (1665–1702) 4th Bt = (1) Dorothy* (1655?–99/1700) dau. of Sir Richard Mason* (2) Henrietta Brett (1681–1718)

'Young' Sir John Brownlow*† (1659–97) 3rd Bt, builder of Belton House = Alice*† (1659–1721)

Savile Cockayne Cust* (1698–1772) of Cockayne Hatley (d.s.p.)

Mary (1679–1718) = Capt. Robert Thompson (1667/8–1711)

Ursula (1683/4–1757) = Richard Newton (d.1737)

Sir Richard Cust* (1680–1734) 2nd Bt of Pinchbeck = Anne* (1694–1779)

William Brownlow*† (1699–1726)

Elizabeth*† (2) (d.1780), dau. of William Cartwright of Marnham = Sir John Brownlow*† (1690–1754) 5th Bt, cr. Viscount Tyrconnel and Baron Charleville 1718, KB 1725 (d.s.p.)

(1) Eleanor*† (1691–1730)

Elizabeth* (1681–1723) = John, 6th Earl of Exeter

Alice* (1684–1727) = Francis, Lord Guilford

Margaret* (1687–1710)

Jane (1689–1736) = Peregrine, 2nd Duke of Ancaster

Lady Elizabeth Cecil* = William Aislabie

Sir John Cust*† (1718–70) 3rd Bt of Pinchbeck and 6th Bt of Humby, Speaker of the House of Commons 1761–70 = Etheldred*† (1720–75) dau. of Thomas Payne of Hough-on-the-hill

Capt. William* (1720–48)

Francis, KC* (1722–91)

Peregrine, MP* (1723–85)

Elizabeth* (1724–69)

Jane* (1725–91)

Richard, DD* (1728–83)

Dorothy* (1729–70)

Lucy* (1732–1804)

Frances* (2) (1756–1847), dau. and heiress of Sir Henry Bankes* of Wimbledon = Sir Brownlow Cust* (1744–1807), 7th Bt, cr. Baron Brownlow 1776 = (1) Jocosa Katerina*† (1748/9–72), dau. of Sir Thomas Drury* of Overstone

Anne = Jacob Reynardson

Elizabeth = Philip Yorke I of Erddig

Sophia*† (1) (1787/8–1814) dau. of Sir Abraham Hume and Amelia*, dau. of John Egerton = John Cust, 2nd Baron Brownlow*† (1779–1853), cr. 1st Earl Brownlow and Viscount Alford 1815 = (2) Caroline† (1793/4–1824), dau. of George Fludyer of Ayston, Rutland* = (3) Emma Sophia* (1792–1872) dau. of 2nd Earl of Mount Edgcumbe

Rev. Henry Cockayne Cust* (1780–1861) of Cockayne Hatley = Anna (d.1866) dau. of 1st Earl of Kilmorey

Rev. Richard* (1785–1864)

Elizabeth Cust

John Hume (Egerton)*† (1812–51), Viscount Alford = Lady Marian Compton*† (1817–88), dau. of 2nd Marquess of Northampton

Charles Henry Brownlow (1813–75)

Henry Francis Cockayne Cust* (1819–84) of Cockayne Hatley = Sara (d.1867), dau. of Isaac Cookson of Meldon, Northumberland

John William Spencer (Egerton Cust)*† (1842–67), 3rd Baron and 2nd Earl Brownlow (d.s.p.)

Adelbert Wellington Brownlow Cust*† (1844–1921), 4th Baron and 3rd and last Earl Brownlow (d.s.p.) = Lady Adelaide Talbot*† (1844/5–1917) dau. of 18th Earl of Shrewsbury

Henry John Cockayne Cust* (Harry Cust) (1861–1917) (d.s.p.) = Emmeline (Nina)* (1867–1955), dau. of Sir William Welby-Gregory of Denton

Adelbert Salusbury Cockayne Cust* (1867–1927), 5th Baron Brownlow = Maud* (d.1936), dau. of Capt. S. Buckle, RE

Elizabeth (d.1913)

Sarah (b.1906)

Peregrine Adelbert Cust* (1899–1978) 6th Baron Brownlow = (1) Katherine* (d.1952) dau. of Brig.-Genl. Sir David Alexander Kinloch, Bart, C.B., M.V.O. = (2) Dorothy Carlotta (1907–66) = (3) Leila

Owners of Belton House appear in **bold type**

* Denotes a portrait in the house

† Denotes a monument in Belton Church

Caroline Elizabeth Maud (b.1928)

David Peregrine Henry Cust (b.1930) (died in infancy)

Edward John Peregrine Cust* (b.1936), 7th Baron Brownlow = Shirlie, dau. of John Yeomans of Hill Croome, Worcs.

Peregrine Edward Quintin Cust (b.1974)

BIBLIOGRAPHY

ANON., 'Belton House', *Country Life*, iv, 1898, pp. 368, 400.

ANON., 'Belton House', *Country Life*. xiv, 1903, p. 614.

ANON. [H. Avray Tipping?], 'Belton House', *Country Life*, xxx, 1911, p. 308.

ANON., 'Furniture of the XVII & XVIII Centuries: Furniture at Belton House', *Country Life*, xxx, 1911, p. 316.

BEARD, Geoffrey, 'Edward Goudge, "The Beste Master in England"', *National Trust Studies*, 1979.

BEARD, Geoffrey, *Craftsmen and Interior Decoration in England 1660–1820*, 1981.

BEARD, Geoffrey, *The Work of Grinling Gibbons*, 1989.

BOLTON, Arthur T., 'Ashridge Park', *Country Life*, l, 1921, pp. 160, 192.

BROWNLOW, Emma Sophia, Countess, *The Eve of Victorianism*, 1940.

BROWNLOW, Emma Sophia, Countess, *Reminiscences of a Septuagenarian*, 1868.

CHRISTIE'S, *Belton House* [catalogue of the sale of the contents, 30 April–2 May 1984].

CORNFORTH, John, 'Belton House', *Country Life*, cxxxvi, 1964, pp. 562, 620, 700.

CORNFORTH, John, and HILL, Oliver, *English Country Houses: Caroline 1625–1685*, 1966.

CORNFORTH, John, *The Search for a Style: Country Life and Architecture 1897–1935*, 1988.

CUST, Lady Elizabeth (ed.), *Records of the Cust Family, Series II: The Brownlows of Belton*, 1909.

CUST, Lionel (ed.)., *Records of the Cust Family, Series III: John Cust, Third Baronet*, 1927.

JACKSON-STOPS, Gervase, *An English Arcadia, 1600–1990*, 1992.

JACQUES, David, *Georgian Gardens, the Reign of Nature*, 1983.

LAING, Alastair, 'Whence this clutch of four?', *Country Life*, clxxxvi, 1991, pp. 172–3 [on the Hondecoeters].

LUMMIS, Trevor, and MARSH, Jan, 'Belton House: Land and Lineage', *The Woman's Domain*, 1990, pp. 34–62.

TINNISWOOD, Adrian, *Historic Houses of the National Trust*, 1991, pp. 141–8.

TIPPING, H. Avray, *English Houses Period IV, Vol I, Late Stuart, 1649–1714*, 1929.

TRIGGS, H. Inigo, *A History of Gardening in England, Wales and Scotland*, 1902.

TURNOR, Edmund, *Collections for the History of the Town and Soke of Grantham*, 1806.

WELLS-COLE, Anthony, *Country House Floors, Temple Newsam*, 1989.

WILCOX, Alfred, *Garden Life*, 24 June 1905.